# Commitment
# to Conquer

# Commitment to Conquer

## Redeeming Your City by Strategic Intercession

### BOB BECKETT

WITH REBECCA WAGNER SYTSEMA

 Chosen Books

A Division of Baker Book House Co
Grand Rapids, Michigan 49516

©1997 by Bob Beckett

Published by Chosen Books
a division of Baker Book House Company
P.O. Box 6287, Grand Rapids, MI 49516-6287

Second printing, May 1998

Printed in the United States of America

### Library of Congress Cataloging-in-Publication Data

Becket, Bob, 1948-
    Commitment to conquer / Bob Beckett with Rebecca Wagner Sytsema.
        p.        cm.
    Includes bibliographical references and index.
    ISBN 0-8007-9252-1 (pbk.)
    1. Spiritual warfare. 2. Pastoral theology. 3. City churches. 4. Powers (Christian theology) 5. Intercessory prayer—Christianity. 6. Beckett, Bob, 1948-    . 7. Hemet Region (Calif.)—Church history—20th century. I. Sytsema, Rebecca Wagner. II. title.
    BV4011.6.B43      1997
    235'.4—dc21                                                97-1373

For information about academic books, resources for Christian leaders, and all new releases available from Baker Book House, visit our web site:
http://www.bakerbooks.com

To my wife, Susan, who has remained my inspiration and encouragement. Without her wisdom and insight, the events of this story would not have been possible.

And to my loving daughters, Sharon Anderson and Susanne Hales, who have been a constant joy and blessing to their father.

# Contents

# Foreword

"He who has an ear, let him hear what the Spirit says to the churches."

Revelation 2:11

Almost any Christian of reasonable maturity is familiar with this statement made by Jesus. He made it not once but fully seven times in Revelation 2–3. Our need to be willing to hear new things from God takes on special urgency in times like these, when changes in the world around us and in the churches we attend are accelerating at a breathtaking pace.

The decade of the 1990s will not tolerate business as usual. The harvest has never been greater, the Kingdom of God has never advanced so rapidly, and for the first time in history a generation has the potential of fulfilling Jesus' Great Commission. Satan's back is against the wall, so to speak, and he has "great wrath, because he knows that he has a short time" (Revelation 12:12). God's armies are on the march, determined as never before to turn nations and people groups "from darkness to light, and from the power of Satan to God" (Acts 26:18). We might expect, therefore, for God to equip His armies with the weapons of warfare appropriate to the task at hand.

This is exactly what He has been doing. Those of us from the more traditional streams of Christianity are becoming aware of some powerful spiritual tools and methodologies that we were not even thinking of ten years ago. We are on a steep (but exciting!) learning curve. The three most significant new spiritual insights that God is providing the Body of Christ in these days are, in my opinion, strategic-level spiritual warfare, spiritual mapping and identificational repentance.

As the decade began, I was privileged to be named coordinator of the International Spiritual Warfare Network. In my task of gathering individuals who had accumulated some knowledge and experience of spiritual warfare, I observed that most of those who came to the meetings were leaders of parachurch ministries such as YWAM, International Fellowship of Intercessors, Generals of Intercession, Every Home for Christ, End-Time Handmaidens and many other such organizations. Very few were practicing local church pastors.

Then Cindy Jacobs introduced me to Pastor Bob Beckett. (The story of the meeting is told later in this book.) When I met Bob, I knew immediately I had found the pearl of great price for which I had been searching: a local church pastor who not only understood strategic-level spiritual warfare, spiritual mapping and identificational repentance, but one who preached these things and, together with his congregation, was putting them energetically into practice in the community to which God had called him. Best of all, I liked the positive, tangible changes taking place in the churches and community of Hemet, California, as an obvious result of the prayers and actions of The Dwelling Place Church, led by Bob and Susan Beckett.

By that time I had begun teaching courses on these subjects at Fuller Seminary and needed a practitioner to balance my role as scholar and theoretician. Bob agreed to help me. I will never forget the day he first came in, toward the end of a one-week intensive course. The students had been fairly well satisfied with what I had given them to that point, but when Bob taught his lesson, it was as if I had plugged the class into a 220-volt outlet. Electricity flowed and sparks were flying everywhere! Then I took the class on a spiritual mapping field trip to Hemet. Never have I seen such enthusiastic evaluations. Even now students refer to that course as "the one when we go to Hemet."

Needless to say, Bob has helped me teach ever since, both on the master's and doctoral levels.

You may not be able to enroll in Fuller Seminary, but you can experience the same electricity by reading this book. *Commitment to Conquer* is the first book to unite the awesome spiritual insights of the 1990s through the eyes and heart of a practicing pastor. His material on how spiritual power is released through sincere commitment to the land and community is one of those groundbreaking, pioneering insights that you will see nowhere else, one that is destined to change the attitudes and ministries of thousands and thousands of pastors across America and around the world.

If you are one of those who have been wondering if all the noise we are hearing these days about spiritual warfare really works, you need look no further. The book you have in your hands will convince you that it does indeed work. Bob Beckett's practical application of strategic-level spiritual warfare, spiritual mapping and identificational repentance has made Hemet the city that, to my knowledge, has experienced the most measurable transformation by the power of the Holy Spirit.

Bob Beckett is one of those who has an ear to hear what the Spirit is saying to the churches. Before you finish this book, you will be hearing those things as well.

*C. Peter Wagner*
*Fuller Theological Seminary*

# Acknowledgments

I would like to acknowledge Ben and Ann Beaird, who took a very lost and lonely young man into their lives and saw him through it all to hear the call; Dick and Betty Mills, who have stood by us over the years with encouragement, support and prayer; and, finally, the staff and congregation of The Dwelling Place, my extended family and friends, where I joyfully carry out that calling.

# Part 1

# A Territorial Commitment

# Hemet Calls!

Any demands that God makes upon us are always logical
and reasonable from God's point of view.

Can a community really be changed? Can the spiritual atmosphere over a city ever be different? Can we as Christians be
used to effect positive changes in schools, reduce drug problems,
decrease gang activity or get pornography off our streets?

The answer is yes! This book is meant to encourage pastors
and laypersons alike who want to see results in their communities. Through commitment to our cities, understanding what is
going on around us and devoting ourselves to prayer, we can see
the Kingdom of God come powerfully into our communities.

## My First Lesson: The Navel of the Earth

The year was 1973. I had come to the Lord only five years
before, during the height of the hippie movement. Although my
background was in engineering, I knew my destiny lay in serving the Lord, so I spent a good deal of those five years training
for the ministry and working with hard-core street kids and drug
addicts.

Now a new challenge faced me—a minimum-security juvenile facility located in the small, searing desert community of Hemet, southwest of Palm Springs in Southern California. My wife, Susan, and I had been asked if we were willing to direct the institution for troubled youngsters.

Move to Hemet, California? At first we did not know. We weighed many factors, trying to balance the pros and cons of such a big change. Finally we decided to give it a try, and packed our bags and headed for our new assignment. I could not have known that the Lord was leading me into a situation far beyond ministry to a group of needy adolescents. In fact, elements about the very property on which the juvenile facility was situated would lead me on a journey that to this day has not ended.

The juvenile facility sat on a 360-acre piece of land adjacent to a reservation for the Soboba Indians. Its view of the foothills of the San Jacinto Mountains was not particularly breathtaking. California live oaks, tangled shrubs, native cactus and drying patches of wild grass mingled among the otherwise dusty hills where the desert fringe met the mountains. It had its own rugged sort of beauty, but the property was not what could be described as inspiring. The land had been owned by a wealthy surgeon who had selected the site especially for training in transcendental meditation.

A man we will call Fred was assigned to show me around the property for the first time. I was interested in the nature of my new surroundings, and had planned to acquaint myself with the land later on, but now I was eager to accept the keys from Fred and get on with my new duties.

But Fred was a talker. He chatted on and on about the property, telling me bits of seemingly nonessential trivia. Then, in the middle of a lengthy discourse, he stopped suddenly. Staring at me with a new sense of purpose, he asked if I would like to see "the navel of the earth."

I had never heard of such a thing. What was it? What would a navel of the earth look like? Fred seemed delighted with my curiosity, and off we tromped to see this unusual sight. If nothing else, I would at least make this man's day.

He proceeded to lead me up a heavily wooded ravine into the mountains. We came to a small box canyon surrounded by natural walls of stone and earth. I could see evidence of a ten-foot waterfall that flowed into the canyon during the rainy season. But this was July, a hot, parched time of year when the stream was dry. No water had flowed here for some months. We entered the canyon from the only possible access, crawling carefully down to the dusty canyon floor. I could see no signs of recent footprints or wildlife within the canyon walls.

Fred's face lit up as he began to explain the significance of this small canyon known as "the navel of the earth." It was an important site, he told me, to those involved in transcendental meditation. Students of the discipline came to this somewhat inaccessible place when water was flowing down the waterfall, to learn how to engage in upper levels of TM.

Under normal circumstances, Fred explained, water fell into the canyon and drained in a clockwise motion. I knew from my background in engineering that this was so. All water above the equator drains clockwise. And the walls of this canyon, as Fred pointed out, had been scarred by the waterfall draining for decades in a clockwise motion. It was easy to see what he meant. But he went on to explain that when the water flowed, those engaging in TM would assume their positions and chant and meditate until the water actually reversed its course and began flowing in a counterclockwise motion!

This, I realized, was impossible. It would be like releasing an apple from a tree and watching it remain aloft, defying the law of gravity.

Fred, seeing my skepticism, challenged me to examine the sediment on the ground of the canyon. I looked down and observed the patterns in the earth. The evidence was clear: The water had indeed drained in a counterclockwise motion.

Looking around once again, I noticed that there were no signs of footprints or wildlife in this canyon since water had last flowed, leaving the place undisturbed. The hair on the back of my neck stood up and a cold shiver ran through my body. Clearly the laws of physics had been broken through use of a mystical spiritual power. But how? And why in this place in particular? An eerie sense seemed to be draped over the canyon and left me with one immediate goal: to get out of there!

After Fred and I had returned safely to the juvenile facility and he had left the property, I began to mull over what he had shown me. Why, if at all, would God want me to know about that unearthly location? What did it mean? I was not sure I believed in all this spooky stuff anyway, and tried to dismiss it from my mind. But despite my best efforts, something of the encounter nagged at me.

As I sat pondering what Fred had shown me, I pulled out a hunting map of the area that I had purchased (since these mountains were replete with deer and other wild game) and located the site of the canyon we had visited. Purely on impulse, I grabbed a red marker and made a small dot at the location Fred had identified as "the navel of the earth."

## More Dots on the Map

During the two years Susan and I spent at the juvenile facility in Hemet, we experienced many bizarre incidents. On several occasions, after locking up the kids for the night, we could hear footsteps in deserted hallways; yet our investigation into the noises proved that no one was there.

And we received many reports of inexplicable apparitions on the property.

### *Footprints in the Field*

I had chosen my office so I could look out onto a field of about three acres that was kept freshly plowed. We used this field as a security device surrounding the grounds. It was kept plowed so that no one could go in or out of the area without leaving footprints in the newly tilled earth.

One day, as I looked across the field, I saw a man standing in the middle of our security acreage. Since we were expecting no visitors, I turned to my desk and called security to inform them of the intruder. Not more than twenty seconds later, I turned back to watch the man from my window—but he was gone.

Some members of security and I went out to investigate. Sure enough, we found a man's footprints just where I had seen the man standing, but we found no sign of footprints coming into or going out of the field.

It was an eerie experience, to say the least. How could a man appear and disappear so quickly? And why were there no footprints in the field, other than where he had been standing? The only explanation was that this had been some kind of apparition.

I decided to add another red mark on my hunting map to show where this strange incident had occurred.

### A Phantom Stagecoach

The neighboring Soboba Indians, whose reservation abutted our property, were deeply entrenched in traditional Native American shamanism. In addition to the shamanistic rituals going on at the reservation, we had seen indications in some of the canyons surrounding our property that animal sacrifices were being made regularly. Evangelistic efforts toward the tribe had produced little, if any, fruit. Darkness seemed to shroud this whole area of the Hemet San Jacinto valley.

Some friends of ours lived on the reservation and reported that at night they often heard what sounded like a stagecoach. They could hear the cadence of multiple hoofbeats at full gallop; the creak of a carriage testing hand-forged hardware; the rocking and rumbling of fast-moving wooden wheels straining beneath their load; and the harsh commands, whistles and crack of a whip as a driver urged his team onward.

There was a history of stagecoaches in the area, but none had run on the road beside our friends' home for many decades. Even so, they reported that, time and time again, the unmistakable sounds of the phantom stagecoach were loud enough to awaken them out of deep sleep.

I marked the location of their home on my map with a red dot.

## New Neighbors

One day as I was in town, I bumped into a friend of mine. As we chatted, he mentioned that some property near Hemet had just been purchased by the Maharishi Mahesh Yogi. The Maharishi himself was apparently planning to make it his home.

This seemed peculiar to me. Why would a senior leader of Hinduism purchase property in this little dirt-water, end-of-the-road town with nothing in particular to offer? After all, here was a man rich enough to settle anywhere he pleased in almost any nation of the world. Why would he come to a small community in a relatively obscure valley in the desert lands of Southern California? I asked the Lord to show me what the Maharishi's attraction to this valley could be.

A little while later, while standing in line at a store in town, I struck up a conversation with a young man who turned out to be one of the Maharishi's own staff members. I took advantage of the opportunity to ask why the land had been purchased and what its intended purpose might be. He told me the Maharishi Yogi felt a unique "aura" in this place, one that would be conducive to practicing deep transcendental meditation.

Hadn't I heard that somewhere before? I ran home and put another red dot on my map indicating the Maharishi's property.

Several months later I received more inside information. This time I met a fellow who served on the staff of L. Ron Hubbard, leader of the Church of Scientology and author of the widely distributed *Dianetics*. The cult leader had just purchased a significant piece of property in the Hemet valley. Why, I asked, was the group interested in this place? Because, he told me, leaders in the Church of Scientology felt "led" to this area.

Within a short time, an impressive complex was constructed that continues, at the time of this writing, to serve as media headquarters for the Church of Scientology. The complex houses a highly sophisticated multimedia facility where all the *Dianetics* commercials and other advertisement propaganda are produced. In addition, the complex has a large campus used as a training institute.

I added another red dot to my map.

And as I marked the Scientology location, I noticed that all the red marks on my map were concentrated in one spot. Why did this area have so much spiritual activity?

## Twelve Men and a Bear Hide

I continued to research the greater Hemet area, noting where strange occurrences, occult activity or sacrifices had taken place. I hiked through all the area canyons, gathering more information and continuing to mark my map. All the lore that I discovered and plotted I kept to myself. No one knew of the unusual hunting map that was slowly becoming a spiritual picture of the valley to which God had called me.

In late 1975 Susan and I resigned our post at the juvenile facility and planted a church in Hemet called Valley Chapel (now known as The Dwelling Place). About that time I received what I can describe only as a vision. I saw, with my eyes wide open, the pelt of a bear spread out over the entire region of the San Jacinto Mountains. It appeared as though a bear hide had been laid over a map of the area, the four paws (still equipped with deadly claws) reaching out in opposing directions—one to the Banning/Beaumont area, one to Palm Springs, one to Anza and one to Hemet. The expanse of the hide covered about thirty square miles, and I could clearly see what appeared to be a backbone running through its center.

Some time later I had the same vision again. Then the occurrences started becoming more frequent, until it seemed that every time I began to pray, I saw the vision. It became disruptive. And it was even more frustrating that I did not know what God was trying to tell me through it.

Finally I cried out to God, asking Him to show me what this vision was and why He kept revealing it to me.

One day I got an answer. Although I heard no audible voice, something in my spirit knew it was the Lord. I sensed that if I took a group of twelve men into the nearby San Jacinto Mountains to pray and fast, God would allow us to break the backbone of the demonic power represented by the bear hide. I would know it was done when I could audibly hear an unusual sound and sense some sort of breaking.

This was downright weird! I had never heard of anything like it before. What made it worse was that I still was not sure I believed in all this stuff. And the toughest part of all was that I had to ask eleven other men to buy into it. But somehow I knew it had to be a directive from the Lord. Those ideas could never have come from within me. I wrestled back and forth with the revelation and finally decided that obedience was better than sacrifice.

So I went to the elders of the church. I did not tell them about the map I had been keeping, but I did tell them about the bear hide and about what I felt the Lord impressing us to do.

The elders did not put me on a forced sabbatical, as I had imagined they might! Instead, these gracious brothers told me that if I received some kind of confirmation, they would be willing to go up the mountain and pray with me.

I relayed the message to the Lord (as if He did not already know!) and left the confirmation completely up to Him. This I had to see!

One morning soon after, I felt a strong impression to visit a store owned by a member of the church. I knew somehow she could show me where to pray concerning the bear hide. I felt awkward, but visited her store as soon as she was open for business.

As I walked in, she looked up. "Ah, Pastor Bob, the Lord told me you were coming!" She reached down behind the counter, grabbed a set of keys and tossed them across the room to me.

"This belongs to my cabin in Idyllwild. Use it as long as you'd like and return the keys when you're done."

I was stunned. Idyllwild was situated in the San Jacinto Mountains right along the backbone on the bear hide on my map.

I thanked her, overwhelmed with gratitude to God, went back to the elders and told them about the cabin. This unusual "coincidence," they agreed, was the confirmation we had sought. We set the time for a week or two later, on a date when everyone could make it, and prepared to see what the Lord would do with twelve men in a cabin He had provided.

On the appointed date, we drove up the mountain in several cars to Idyllwild. We shared an air of anticipation as we settled into the cabin. Then, for hours into the night, we prayed and fasted. Anticipation of a spiritual battle was replaced slowly by weariness of flesh. At about three in the morning, I felt I was fighting sleep more than anything else.

Suddenly I sensed a change. Thick, heavy darkness descended over the cabin. The difference from one moment to the next was palpable. All my fatigue disappeared. Something more powerful than the twelve of us guys permeated the atmosphere of the cabin like a noxious blanket of gas. Without any one of us leading out, we all launched into the old hymn "Power in the Blood."

There we sat under heavy oppression in a mountain cabin, singing to the best of our ability, when we heard a popping noise. The crack, loud enough to be audible over twelve men's voices, sounded like a joint between two bones popping out of place, much like the cracking of mammoth knuckles. At that point, to our astonishment, the cabin actually began to shake. Our singing became louder, even desperate, as the earth beneath us trembled.

Suddenly there was calm and quiet. The oppressive presence was gone. Peace flooded us and we knew we were safe.

As our caravan of vehicles headed down the mountain that morning, I had little clue as to what had just happened. But I knew we had accomplished what the Lord had sent us there to do.

After our bizarre mountaintop adventure, the church experienced a spurt of growth. Greater numbers of people came to the Lord. The pastors of the city were more willing to work with the other pastors in the community. Something over Hemet did seem different. What had happened at the cabin? Was there something more God wanted to show us through all this?

My church knew about the bear hide and the cabin, but no one, not even the elders, knew of the map I had been keeping— peppered now with red dots, each bearing some kind of spiritual significance. And so it went for fifteen years.

## The Map Revealed

Then in 1992 The Dwelling Place hosted a spiritual warfare conference at which my good, long-time friend Cindy Jacobs was speaking. C. Peter Wagner, a professor at Fuller Theological Seminary whose ministry I respected highly, had also agreed to speak.

For days leading up to the meeting, the map had nagged me. Was there anything to it? Had God really been leading me to keep the map all these years? If so, what significance did it have? I decided it was time to tell someone about it.

The night before the conference, Cindy brought Peter and his wife, Doris, to our home so Susan and I could get acquainted with them. I pulled Cindy aside, showed her the map and explained what each red dot signified.

Cindy, who had been involved for some time in praying for cities and nations, thought the map was a significant document showing what Satan had been doing in the area. She encouraged me to show it to Peter. But did I dare show a respected seminary professor such a wild map on our first meeting? Would he consider me out on the lunatic fringe? Would I be committing professional suicide?

Only later did I learn that Peter, in the few years prior to this conference, had been researching the area of spiritual warfare as it related to church growth. In 1989 Peter, Doris and Cindy had attended a major consultation on world evangelization in Manila called Lausanne II Congress on World Evangelization. At that consultation, five workshops had been dedicated to the field of spiritual warfare. Peter, one of the workshop leaders, had presented the concept of *territorial spirits*—demonic ruling principalities—to Christian leaders of all denominations. It was possibly the first time in history that such a workshop had been presented. Out of that meeting, Peter and Cindy, along with Charles Kraft and Gary Clark, convened a group of people who had studied or practiced spiritual warfare in the United States. It was called the Spiritual Warfare Network and had already gathered twice by the time I met Peter.

Not knowing any of this, I was reluctant to lay out my unusual map to him. But summoning my courage, I asked Peter and Doris if I could share some things about the Hemet area with them. Then I spread my well-worn map on the dining room table and explained in great detail what I had been learning about the region. I told them how the map got started. I shared the history of each of the numerous dots. For some 45 minutes I laid out the story piece by piece.

During all this time, Peter did not say a word. Nothing in his facial expression even changed. By story's end I was sweating bullets!

When I was finally finished pouring my heart out, setting fifteen years of my secret before this man, I found the nerve to ask what he thought. There was momentary silence as he stared at the map. Then he shifted slightly in his chair and crossed his arms over his chest. My heart was pounding wildly.

Finally he looked up and asked, "Have you heard of *The Lonesome Gods* by Louis L'Amour?"

What kind of response was that? It took me a moment to remember that Louis L'Amour was a renowned Western novelist. I had never read any of his books. Westerns did not interest me. At this moment they interested me even less!

With no clue as to what Peter was talking about, and beginning to wonder if he had heard a thing I had said, I answered, "No, I've never heard of it."

"Well," said Peter, "I think you should read it. There might be something in there that can help you with this."

Peter, as it turned out, was a big fan of Louis L'Amour novels. He told me L'Amour had gained his fame by studying a region and its history thoroughly, then basing a fictitious story around well-documented facts. *The Lonesome Gods* was set in the San Jacinto Mountains where I had been mapping. He wondered if some of the research in that novel could help me understand the spiritual history of my region.

Frankly, the last thing I had the time or desire to do was read a Western novel. Wanting to submit to authority, however, I got a copy of *The Lonesome Gods* the very next day.

The back cover promoted the book as L'Amour's "biggest and most important historical novel to date." Biggest was certainly true; the story itself was 450 pages! Was there something prophetic about its being his "most important historical novel to date"? I hoped so.

As I delved into the book, I realized Peter was right. The novel, which took me about 36 hours to devour, offered me a wealth of historical information I had not known about.

Throughout the book I noticed one specific name, *Tahquitz,* coming up over and over. It was a name I had heard before and given little thought to. Now I learned that *Tahquitz* means "the Evil One." The native peoples of the region revered the spirit of Tahquitz and believed it resided someplace in the San Jacinto Mountains.

When I finished the book, I sensed the Spirit of the Lord saying, *Get out the map and find Tahquitz.*

As I pulled out the map and found Tahquitz, I realized that the cabin we had prayed in fifteen years before was located on the mountain leading to Tahquitz. In fact, that cabin was one of the highest cabins on the mountain, and if you walked out the back door, you would be faced with a thousand-foot rock spire called Tahquitz Peak. It was located right along the back-bone of the bear hide I had seen in the recurring vision. In fact, it had been where we heard the popping sound.

Fifteen years prior, we had been sent by God to that cabin to do strategic-level spiritual warfare, without a clue as to what we were doing. I was amazed now to go back to the book and reread Louis L'Amour's description:

> Tahquitz is supposed to be an evil spirit. Some say he's a mon-ster of some kind, even a dragon. Once in a while the mountains rumble and they say Tahquitz is trying to escape.[1]

I thought back to when, on that mountain, the cabin began to shake. Could it be that the spirit of Tahquitz was the one being dislodged?

In any case, I knew for the first time since 1973 that God was really saying something with this map. I called Peter Wagner that afternoon (since the conference was over) and faxed him a copy of the map showing the location of Tahquitz Peak. He agreed: The mysterious trek I had been on all these years had truly been led by the Lord. Now more than ever I felt compelled to stay on it and see where it led.

## An Adventure Far from Over

It has been an exciting adventure for me and for many of the pastors in this community. As we have learned to use the his-torical and geographical information we have gleaned, and as we have learned about accurate intercession, we have seen re-markable changes take place in our region. I firmly believe that many of the results you will see in the following pages can occur in *any* community.

God has allowed you and me to live in one of the most excit-ing times for Christians in all of history. Never have we seen a greater harvest than today. Never have we had the tools we now have to see cities changed by the Spirit of God.

Even so, the warfare we must face is greater than at any time before. This level of spiritual combat requires a careful understanding—particularly on the part of pastors—of the commitment God has called us to within our cities. I hope that as you read the rest of this book, whether you are a pastor or a layperson, you will gain new understanding and a greater sense of destiny into God's desire for you and the place to which He has called you. May the cry of every believer in every community be, "Your Kingdom come, Your will be done in my city as it is in heaven."

# 2

# Maximizing the Power of Intercession

*You'll never be too small to serve your community, only too big; never too dumb, only too smart; never too poor, only too rich; never too inept, only too clever.*

In my early days of pastoring The Dwelling Place, I grew to love my community. The Lord took me through the process of making a serious commitment to the Hemet area (a commitment I will share more about in chapter 4). My strongest desire was to see the Kingdom of God come in greater ways into our valley. I wanted to see an alleviation of our drug and gang problems. The Native American population in and around our community needed a touch from God. The serious problem of pornography needed to be dealt with. On and on went the list of typical problems that most communities to some degree face.

How could our small, local church make any difference? Only a move of God would really change our city. So we decided to employ the strongest weapon of spiritual warfare: prayer.

We were learning at the time about the increasingly popular concept of "Could You Not Tarry One Hour?" that had been introduced to the Body of Christ by Larry Lea. This tremendous teaching made so much sense to us that we decided to institute a church-wide corporate prayer meeting. Using Lea's model, we began meeting every weekday between six and seven in the morning.

We were faithful to our commitment. For five solid years, five days a week, our church prayed every morning for one hour. Depending on the circumstances of the day, we had anywhere from ten to one hundred people at those meetings. We prayed our hearts out about drugs, gangs, schools, pornography—all the issues that concerned our community. We came against the works of Satan. We bound spirits left and right.

Meanwhile, the lives of those who came regularly were changed. My own prayer life was altered dramatically. As a church we learned the invaluable discipline of coming together faithfully before the Lord. We became a tight-knit family who shared one another's burdens and poured our hearts out in prayer for our community.

The only problem was, at the end of those five years of faithful intercession, totaling about 1,300 hours of corporate prayer, Hemet had not changed one bit. In fact, if anything it was worse. While I praised the Lord for what our meetings had accomplished in individual lives and in our church, I remained frustrated at our lack of effectiveness beyond our four walls. What could the problem be? How could we be armed with a weapon as powerful as prayer and not have made progress in the war?

## Scud Missile or Smart Bomb Praying?

I went to the Lord earnestly seeking answers. And gradually He began to show me what our problem was. Although we had been interceding faithfully, our intercession had not been persistently accurate. We had simply sprayed prayers here and there, hoping they would hit a target.

I analyzed the scenario of our typical morning prayer meeting. We would come in a little before six each morning, coffee cups in hand, and chat for a few minutes. When six o'clock came we would get revved up for prayer. We knew what we wanted to see changed, so we would start in. Take the issue of drugs. We would pray against drug problems. We would pray against drug dealers. We would pray against all drugs everywhere. We would bind spirits of drugs affecting our community. Then, in all honesty, we would get tired of praying about drugs, so we would move on to something else and do the same thing.

Now, after five years, I felt the Lord saying that just when we were about to have a breakthrough, we would allow boredom to set in and move on prematurely.

How could 1,300 hours of prayer not have made a significant impact on our community? In part because we really did not know exactly what we were praying about. Since we were praying without accurate information, we had no way of evaluating our progress.

It is a fact of life that no matter what you are trying to accomplish, if you have no way to evaluate your progress, the boredom factor will eventually come into play. If you can find out what is happening as a result of your efforts, however, your motivation, fervency and end results will be far greater.

The most poignant analogy of what we as a church were doing came during the Gulf War, when I watched CNN in my living room. I could just imagine Saddam Hussein getting up one morning during the war in a bad mood, his hatred for Israel particularly strong. After getting dressed and taking care of some dictatorial matters over breakfast, his first act of business would be ordering a missile strike against Israel. His generals would scurry to carry out their commander's wishes. Orders would flow down the ranks until the unit in charge of the now-famous scud missiles would prepare for a launch. They would point their missile launcher in the general direction of Israel, calculate wind velocity and fire.

When the report that a missile had been launched would come back through the ranks to Saddam's command center, he had no way of knowing what his missile would hit. Later we learned that Saddam actually turned on CNN to find out what his missiles were striking. It chilled me to realize that if the scud had been an accurate weapon, the war might have turned out very differently.

But our praying was just as inaccurate. Our spray of intercession might or might not hit the target we hoped for as we geared up for prayer. We were willing and able to strike but lacked the capacity for accuracy. The Dwelling Place needed new results from prayer if we were ever to make a difference in our city. I had to come to grips with making some changes. (A definition of insanity spoke to us in our situation: doing something the same way you have always done it but expecting to see new results!)

If we could add the element of accurate intercession to the prayer life of our church, I was convinced our community would begin to improve. Again, the Gulf War offered a model. The bombs of the Allied forces knew their exact targets and, for the most part, destroyed specific buildings or sites—nothing more, nothing less. Why could these so-called smart bombs hit their targets so accurately? It was because coordinates had been programmed within them. How did the Allied forces know which coordinates to use? Because of reconnaissance information that had been gathered behind enemy lines. Even smart bombs would have no effect without the amassing of strategic information behind enemy lines to render the enemy helpless.

That, I thought, is how our intercession should be. We knew the value of prayer. We knew how to bind demonic forces. We were willing to put in the time and energy. We did not have enough understanding, however, of what our enemy was doing to hold Hemet in bondage. We did not know how to aim our prayers in such a way as to destroy Satan's strongholds—fortresses that exist both in the mind and in particular locations.

The first thing we had to do was find out the Lord's agenda for our community. What was it He wanted us to tackle in our warfare praying? How were we to approach various problems? What was God's highest priority in our town? If we wanted to see His Kingdom come and His will be done in Hemet, we needed to know what His will was.

Then, once we determined God's plan for our community, we had to find a way of evaluating our progress, some way to look at each problem and see if the powers of darkness were losing their hold. If we were not making headway in an area we knew the Lord had called us to pray over, we would know to persevere in our warfare and not move on prematurely.

An understanding of "smart bomb praying"—prayers armed with warheads of specific information regarding issues of darkness within our community—moved us into strategic-level intercession, delivering smart bomb prayers on behalf of a geographical location (in our case, Hemet). And as The Dwelling Place moved toward accurate, strategic-level praying, we began to find out what really—and I mean *really*—was going on in our city.

The Lord revealed more and more to us as we prayed. Because we knew where problems had the greatest grip and why those areas were more affected, we learned what we were hitting with our prayers. After a while, when we prayed, we could go back and evaluate our progress. If we did not see significant changes, we knew to go back and pray some more.

Eventually we started seeing breakthroughs in our community. Nothing has fulfilled me more as a pastor than watching this city I love so dearly become more infiltrated with the Kingdom of God. And as you will see in the testimonies throughout the rest of this book, God allowed us to arrive at the place were we could employ smart bomb strategies in our intercession.

## Spiritual Mapping: Hidden Things Revealed

Strategic-level intercession is what Paul referred to in Ephesians 6:12 when he told us,

> We do not wrestle against flesh and blood, but against principalities, against powers, against the rulers of the darkness of this age, against spiritual hosts of wickedness in the heavenly places.

The beings described here are the forces Satan uses to maintain strongholds over a given area. The "wrestling" referred to is the strategic-level intercession God's people can do to see the principalities and powers neutralized. (I will talk more about ways to do this, including identificational repentance, solemn assemblies and prophetic prayer acts, in Parts 2 and 3.)

In order to conduct smart bomb praying and strategic-level intercession, we must first do spiritual mapping—researching an area historically to determine how darkness has gained legitimate access to the region. And in order to wage war on darkness, some reconnaissance is needed, just as it was in the Gulf War.

Many cities, like people, have beautifully painted facades with something entirely different going on inside. Some of the loveliest homes in a city may be dens of witchcraft. High-class restaurants can be fronts for drugs. The goal of spiritual mapping is to find out what is going on in the secret, hidden places.

In mapping a city or community, we must prepare ourselves, first by calling on the Lord, and then by allowing Him to give us the spiritual eyes to see hidden things revealed. Jeremiah 33:3 (AMP) says,

> "Call to Me and I will answer you and show you great and mighty things, fenced in and hidden, which you do not know—do not distinguish and recognize, have knowledge of and understand."

Would you like to see the hidden things in your community? Through the power of God they can be revealed. But it is important to remember to call to God, as the prophet Jeremiah admonished us, who alone can show us how to make our intercession accurate.

In 2 Corinthians 4:18 Paul wrote,

> We do not look at the things which are seen, but at the things which are not seen. For the things which are seen are temporary, but the things which are not seen are eternal.

Undoubtedly Paul was referring to things of the spirit—souls, forces, principalities, powers—that lie behind what we see with our natural eyes. These are the clues we seek as we begin the process of mapping a community. Unfortunately, unless we are looking with spiritual vision, we cannot see the spiritual forces at work behind what we can see with our eyes.[1]

Here is a way to start becoming more sensitive to what lies behind the everyday workings of your community. Those who have been involved in spiritual mapping agree there are three crucial questions we must ask:

1. What is wrong in my community?
2. How did my community get that way?
3. What can I do about things as they are?

While we will explore in later chapters how to answer these questions and understand our own communities, let's take a brief look at each of the questions now.

### 1. What Is Wrong in Our Community?

The main objective of spiritual mapping, as we have noted, is to discover the hidden things within a community. Often this is where a physical map may come into play, like the hunting map I used when I first moved to Hemet. Once I realized the Lord had led me to keep the map, I studied it with new eyes. The red markings I had made seemed, strangely enough, to come in clusters, showing where darkness was greater. I could see what kinds of problems faced our community based on what each of those marks represented.

As our church became more knowledgeable about spiritual mapping, our techniques became more sophisticated. Today we have a "war room" in our church. This war room is not open to the public. Only proven intercessors who have obtained permission are allowed to use it for prayer. One wall of our war room is covered with a huge map of our city. As the face of our community changes, so does the map. Recognized intercessors can pray over our community at any time. This map has become an important tool for us to see what the city of Hemet is like and how it is changing.

## 2. How Did Our Community Get That Way?

We will go much deeper into this subject in Part 2 of this book, but I cannot overstate that an area is shaped by its history. History may be the most important part of spiritual mapping. It answers the question as to how our community has become what it is today. Only in mapping the history of a city can we understand its strongholds—places that export darkness and repel light.

Events that occurred hundreds of years ago can still have an effect on communities today. Just as traits are passed through family lines, so are they passed through the generations of a city. It is crucial to know who founded the city and why, and what happened to the original people of the land (in our case, the Native Americans). All the facts that make up dusty old history books are the foundation on which the current situation of any region is built. Unless we understand what has gone before, any efforts we make at intercession for our communities will comprise only scud missile-type praying.

## 3. What Can We Do about Things as They Are?

Once we have gained clear understanding of the problems and history of a community, the heart of God for that city will often begin to emerge, and we will see clearly what needs to be changed. Perhaps one city must deal with apathy toward the Gospel. Maybe another city has great wealth but close-fisted people. Other communities may be gripped by strongholds of religion, sectarianism, gambling or prostitution.

Through physical and historical mapping, we can begin to understand what keeps a community in bondage. Now is the time to pray. Information available through the use of mapping will enable intercessory prayers to hit their targets with precision.

## Our Ultimate Objective

Believers are given to strategic-level prayer not to know more secrets about our cities, and not simply to have greater insight into the works of Satan within our communities. In fact, we are interested in what our enemy is up to only as it relates to the purposes of God being established. Let the cry of our hearts be, "Your Kingdom come, Your will be done in my city as it is in heaven."

But what does that really mean?

### *Activating the Church*

Isaiah 61:1–3 says,

> "The Spirit of the Lord GOD is upon Me, because the Lord has anointed Me to preach good tidings to the poor; He has sent Me to heal the brokenhearted, to proclaim liberty to the captives, and the opening of the prison to those who are bound; to proclaim the acceptable year of the LORD, and the day of vengeance of our God; to comfort all who mourn, to console those who mourn in Zion, to give them beauty for ashes, the oil of joy for mourning, the garment of praise for the spirit of heaviness; that they may be called trees of righteousness, the planting of the LORD, that He may be glorified."

The prophet Isaiah was foretelling the works of Jesus. Centuries later the Carpenter from Nazareth astounded those in the synagogue when, after reading these phrases, He announced that this prophecy had been fulfilled in their hearing (see Luke 4:16–21).

How much greater are the works the Lord desires to accomplish through His Church today? All the activities listed by Isaiah are manifestations of the Kingdom of God. And Satan hates them! He will do whatever he can to thwart the works of God.

We stop painfully short of the ultimate goal of strategic-level intercession and spiritual mapping if we simply pray against the enemy's plots within a city. We must also pray fervently for the fruitful things of God to enter the situation. Jeremiah 1:10 reminds us that our job is not only "to root out and to pull down, to destroy and to throw down," but also "to build and to plant." As the powers of darkness are neutralized, the Church can get on with the work God has called us to do.

### *Eternal Fruit*

The greatest mandate the Lord left believers was to make disciples of all nations (see Matthew 28:19–20). There is nothing Satan holds onto with greater vengeance than an unsaved soul. He would much sooner see a Christian healed or a demon cast out than he would a soul saved. Why? Because healing or deliverance does not have eternal impact. Even a body healed by Jesus eventually dies. Personal deliverance is also temporal. But a soul saved is a permanent, eternal victory for the Kingdom of God.

This is the pivotal point on which all spiritual warfare is waged. Never, never should we engage the enemy as an end in itself. The primary proof for testing the effectiveness of strategic-level prayer is simple: Are new names being written in the Lamb's Book of Life?

We will see other evidences of the Kingdom of God in the process, of course. The sick will be healed. The demonized will be freed. People committing all kinds of sin will repent. All these things are good and signify victories in the battle. But nothing is sweeter in the sight of God than seeing a soul for whom He sacrificed His only Son turn away from the kingdom of darkness and accept the salvation offered freely, forever to be in communion with Him. This is the ultimate objective and absolute purpose for any strategic-level intercession.

## No Longer Just Theory

During the years I kept my map in secret, I thought I was alone. No one else in the world, I thought, had ever conceived such a notion. How wrong I was! Many others throughout the world were learning the same lessons, although I did not find out how the Lord had been moving until early 1990.

In the nation of Sweden, for example, God directed a man who can be called a pioneer in the field of spiritual mapping. As leader of Intercessors for Sweden, Kjell Sjoberg was in a unique position to lead an army of prayer warriors in battle for that nation, and he is among the first of our generation to become involved in this kind of spiritual espionage.[2]

In Guatemala a young lawyer accepted the Lord and turned his heart toward ministry. Harold Caballeros, who later became the founding pastor of El Shaddai Church, discovered many strongholds of the enemy as the Lord led him through a similar mapping process. Today Guatemala is one of the nations most receptive to the Gospel, due in part to the mapping and fervent intercession of warriors at El Shaddai.

During the time I was making notations on my map, a young parachurch leader was gathering thousands of pages of spiritual information on the strongholds of arguably the darkest region of the world—the one controlled by Islam. George Otis, Jr., perhaps the foremost authority in the field of spiritual mapping, was being sent by the Lord into areas that few dare to tread. As a result Otis wrote *The Last of the Giants* (Chosen Books, 1991), considered by some the textbook to date on spiritual mapping in areas most resistant to the Gospel.

In Argentina Victor Lorenzo was led by the Lord to expose high-level schemes of the enemy in the cities of La Plata and Resistencia. Ed Silvoso worked with Victor as he learned how Satan had used these cities. This information, incorporated into a larger plan for taking cities for Jesus Christ, helped produce vibrant results. Now the town of Resistencia is used as a model for strategic city-taking through prayer evangelism. After 1990, Ed Silvoso reports, the Church in Resistencia grew "over 500 percent, and the total number of congregations [grew to] 200, an increase of 130 new ones."[3] Resistencia is a prime example of eternal fruit born out of strategic-level warfare.

I mentioned in the last chapter that in 1989, Peter Wagner, Cindy Jacobs, Charles Kraft and Gary Clark convened a group in the United States, following the Lausanne II Congress on World Evangelization in Manila, for strategic-level warfare that included the field of spiritual mapping. Notable leaders such as David Bryant, John Dawson, Joy Dawson, Dick Eastman, Larry Lea, Dick Bernal, Jane Hansen, Francis Frangipane, Ed Murphy, Tom White, George Otis, Jr., Ed Silvoso, B. J. Willhite, Gwen Shaw and many others (including me) gathered with the conveners to form the Spiritual Warfare Network. Those in the Network quickly realized we needed one another for wisdom, encouragement, correction, intercession, partnership in ministry and cross-fertilization of ideas. As a group we found ourselves providing balance, accountability and protection to one another in a field particularly vulnerable to excesses.

As the Spiritual Warfare Network took shape over the next two years, it began to expand outside the United States. Today the Spiritual Warfare Network has regional coordinators throughout the world who identify those within their assigned regions whom God has called into strategic-level spiritual warfare and mapping for the purpose of evangelization.

Those who move into this field need not be lone rangers. God is moving in His Church throughout the world to teach us new concepts and equip us with tools and weapons that cause our prayers to be effective battering rams against the forces of hell. These forces are keeping people captive and preventing them from reconciliation with their Creator through Jesus Christ. It is important to know that the Lord has called many into this process as He is redeeming lost souls into His heavenly Kingdom.

## What about Small and Medium-Sized Churches?

This is just a glimpse of what the Lord is doing in the world. Now let's bring it home to where you and I live. How easy it is to read the names of prominent leaders God has called into the field of strategic-level intercession and feel a sense of inadequacy. This is especially true for pastors of small congregations whose main concern is keeping their families fed.

Nonetheless, there is some good news for pastors of small or medium-sized churches who want to make a difference outside the church walls. Such pastors are a unique piece of the puzzle God is putting together in many communities. In fact, they are spiritual gatekeepers in their cities (more on that in chapters 9 and 10). Strategic-level intercession is not only a mega-church endeavor. If you feel called by God to enter this level of warfare, even though your church is not large, be encouraged. Strategic-level intercession is still for you.

As a pastor, I have noticed that many of my friends in leadership positions go to conferences led by mega-church pastors who often talk in terms of mega-church influence. It can be frustrating to realize the presenters may have more secretaries than you have people! Don't get me wrong. There is nothing bad about these seminars. It is just that the enemy will use whatever means he can to make pastors think that until their churches are large, they cannot be a force in their communities.

Don't get caught in that trap. Strategic-level intercession can take a small or medium-sized church and turn it into a mega-force within a city. In my case, even though The Dwelling Place has grown considerably, I came to grips quite some time ago with the understanding that having a big church is not a prerequisite to having a big impact on your community. But if you want to make a greater impact on your community, you may well end up with a big church as a result. I am content in this knowledge and feel fulfilled pastoring in the community to which God has called me. My heart is for lost souls rather than for a big church. And God has blessed us richly.

And with the use of smart bomb praying, I believe The Dwelling Place has been and will be used by God to make a significant impact on the Hemet area. Great things for the Lord often come in small packages. When we are led by the Holy Spirit, these principles can turn a small church into a force to be reckoned with.

## Mapping Is Not Magic

The concept of smart bomb praying may get you excited. It should! Prayer is the most powerful weapon given to us by the Holy Spirit; and even more powerful are prayers targeted at the heart of darkness. But these are not a magic formula by which we can somehow manipulate supernatural forces to comply with our agendas. The power flows from the throne of God. We must see ourselves as vessels used by the Lord to further His Kingdom where we live.

Because this field is particularly subject to flakiness, I would like to share some honest concerns and cautions that may help pastors and lay people alike to avoid snares of excess or presumption. Here are some basic issues to consider before engaging in this level of intercession:

### 1. Don't Get Involved If Your Church Does Not Have a Heart for Intercession

Spiritual mapping will never produce results without intercession. In fact, mapping will only cause heartache if a pastor is not willing to lead the church into true strategic-level intercession. Satan's main strength is working through occult methods (defined by Webster as "hidden from view, or secret"). Forces of darkness work hard to keep their movements undetected by God's people. Churches that become involved in strategic-level intercession and spiritual mapping can expect an increase of opposition from the enemy.

Does that mean the pastor must have the gift of intercession personally? No. But pastors must have those within their congregations who do have the gift and a God-given desire to intercede fervently.

### 2. Don't Get Involved If You Don't Have a Heart for the Community

If you as a pastor or layperson have not made a commitment to the community in which you live, this is probably the wrong path for your church. Moving beyond the walls of your sanctuary may not be your priority. If that is the case, don't get involved in spiritual mapping or strategic-level intercession. But please don't stop reading. I want to encourage you to consider some of the questions and challenges I will raise in chapters 3 and 4.

### 3. Spiritual Mapping Is Not for Everyone

The concept of spiritual mapping will stir curiosity in some and skepticism in others. That's all right. I fully believe in finding out what we are good at, both as individuals and as churches, and concentrating on those things.

It amazes me how beautifully the Body of Christ is put together! Here in Hemet the pastors of the city have experienced a tremendous sense of unity. I marvel at how God has fit us together, each church with its own giftings and specialties. God has not called every church in this city to strategic-level intercession. In fact, the percentage of churches involved in this is low. Still, I see Hemet as a model of how the Body of Christ works together, something I will elaborate on throughout this book.

It is legitimate *not* to plunge into strategic-level spiritual warfare simply because God has not called your church to do so, and this in no way reflects on your desire for intercession or your heart for the community.

### 4. Don't Be a Renegade Intercessor

One of the most dangerous things in the Body of Christ, particularly in the area of strategic-level warfare, is intercessors who are simply uninformed or who insist on doing their own thing. Moving out alone can be dangerous for the intercessor and is usually ineffective in the city. I cannot count how many times I have heard from intercessors who feel their lives are in a shambles because they moved in presumption. Often these dear brothers and sisters received legitimate insights into principalities and powers over a city but felt compelled to use this information by going out alone and praying against a principality or power. Don't ever do this. This is not a game. This is war. Lives are literally at stake.

If you feel you have received insight from the Lord about a stronghold in your area, share it with your pastor or a leader of a prayer team. Test it. Submit it to someone in authority. If the Lord has revealed something to you, He will not mind confirming it, and it will stand up over time. But before you act on it, discern clearly what the Lord wants you to do with the information.

### 5. Spiritual Mapping Is Not Another Fad or Movement; It Is a Lifestyle

If you feel that the Lord may be calling you to spiritual mapping, understand that this is not another church program. It is a lifestyle. Be prepared to make some changes. But in making those changes and answering God's call, prepare for the exciting things God wants to bring about within your city!

Now let's look at the first step in taking spiritual possession of your community.

# The Earth Is the Lord's

You can't solve a problem with the same thinking that caused it.

Albert Einstein

Every once in a while I find myself swept away by the utter beauty of creation around me. The brilliant oranges of a late summer sunset reflected exquisitely in the billows of a boundless ocean. A towering waterfall thundering from a cliff toward pools below. A myriad of greens bursting into new life as the last snows of winter melt into spring. These and countless other images speak of the awesome creation of God. "The earth is the LORD's, and all its fullness, the world and those who dwell therein" (Psalm 24:1).

In every season, in every place created by God, we find beauty. Why is that? Because God has put something of Himself in all creation. Whether you love the country or the bustle of the city, certain things probably strike a chord of appreciation in you for the care He took in creating so splendid a world for us to enjoy.

He enjoys it, too. In fact, as we tackle the field of spiritual mapping, let's look first at how God views territory and land.

## Does God Love Soil?

The human race is not the only object of God's affection. We are indeed the primary objects of His love here on earth, but not the exclusive recipients. Of course, God created us, the human race, in His image. His love for us runs so deep that He sacrificed His only Son so we could be reconciled to Him.

Nevertheless, God also loves the land He has created. He cares about actual, physical soil and what comes forth from that soil.

This may be a new thought to you. Consider, however, that while God created light with a mere command, He took far more time to fashion the earth. He created seas, land, flora, fauna and seasons with great care. Nothing in creation was made haphazardly. It was with divine order and balance that the Lord poured Himself into the creation of the earth. Romans 1:20 says:

> Since the creation of the world His invisible attributes are clearly seen, being understood by the things that are made, even His eternal power and Godhead, so that they are without excuse.

God's tender care for us and for the earth is evidenced in the beauty of the earth itself.

As history unfolded and the human population grew, God set boundaries for the nations of the earth on the precious land He had created. As people groups began to form, each became associated with a geographical location:

> He has made from one blood every nation of men to dwell on all the face of the earth, *and has determined their preappointed times and the boundaries of their habitation.*
>
> Acts 17:26 (italics added)

Since the time of Adam, God has been busy distributing the peoples of the earth throughout the continents and islands He fashioned as their dwelling places. Indeed, He created every nation, province, territory and city for His own purposes.

But just as Satan set about to pervert God's first and best plan for humankind, he also set about to pervert God's first and best plan for the land over which He gave human beings dominion.

## The Edenic Covenant

Let me share some of my own personal theology concerning the Lord's love for the land and why this love is so important in His ultimate redemptive purpose.

The Bible is clear about the God-given responsibility the human race has for the land. From the time of Adam, care for the land has fallen on the shoulders of humankind. To better understand this great responsibility, let's go back to Genesis to see, from the story of creation and the dawning of the human race, what God intended.

Even before there was an Adamic covenant, there was an Edenic covenant. The very first interaction God had with Adam, after breathing life into his inanimate form, was to set him within Eden in order for Adam to tend the Garden:

> The LORD God formed man of the dust of the ground, and breathed into his nostrils the breath of life; and man became a living being. . . . Then the LORD God took the man and put him in the garden of Eden to tend and keep it.
>
> Genesis 2:7, 15

Bible scholar C. I. Scofield noted about this passage:

> A covenant is a sovereign pronouncement of God by which He establishes a relationship of responsibility between Himself and an individual (e.g., Adam in the Edenic Covenant, Gen. 2:16ff.).[1]

Before giving Adam any further instruction, even before giving him Eve, God established that Adam's responsibility was to tend the Garden of Eden. In return God would provide, through the Garden, Adam's need for food and a home. Adam's nourishment would come from the fruit of the trees of the Garden, and any shelter from the physical makeup of the land. This was the substance of the Edenic covenant, or "relationship of responsibility."

In this covenant the Lord was *geographically* specific in the instructions He gave Adam. He did not give Adam the whole world to tend. He did not even assign a surrounding region to Adam's care. God required Adam only to tend the Garden that was within the region of Eden. Before the Fall, God associated Adam with the Garden, and it was there that He would come to speak with him.

So the Edenic covenant represented Adam's commitment to the land in which God had called him to dwell.

## Obedience Removed, Obedience Redeemed

In the course of events, Adam was disobedient to the one restriction the Lord had placed on him. As a result of his sin, a breach occurred between humans and God that was irreparable without the blood of Jesus.

When Adam ate the fruit of the tree of the knowledge of good and evil, the consequences of his action extended far beyond human alienation from the Creator. Locked up within that act of original sin was the removal of obedience, not only from humankind, but also from the earth. So long as the fruit had remained on the tree, Adam was obedient. But when "the fruit of that forbidden tree" (in Milton's words) was plucked from its branches, the divine connection between heaven and earth was severed.

Not only did God's relationship with humans change; His relationship to the land changed, too. In fact, part of the punishment the Lord pronounced on Adam entailed a curse on the land. God told Adam:

> "Cursed is the ground for your sake; in toil you shall eat of it all
> the days of your life. Both thorns and thistles it shall bring forth

for you, and you shall eat the herb of the field. In the sweat of
your face you shall eat bread till you return to the ground, for out
of it you were taken; for dust you are, and to dust you shall return."
Genesis 3:17b–19

But God, in His infinite wisdom and mercy, had a plan to
redeem not only human beings but the land that had become
cursed for Adam's sake. Obedience had been removed from the
earth by the first Adam. But when the second Adam placed Himself on the sacred tree—that is, when Christ died on the cross—
obedience was returned to the earth.

What does it mean to say that obedience was removed from
the earth through a tree and returned to the earth through a tree?
Can I possibly be suggesting that there is some significance in
trees?

Let's look once again at Romans 1:20: "Since the creation of
the world His invisible attributes are clearly seen, being understood by the things that are made. . . ." We could argue, based
on this verse, that everything on earth created by God is patterned
after something in the spirit realm. Nothing created by God lacks
spiritual significance. Everything is intended to be a picture of
some divine attribute.

Within our Western worldview, this concept may seem at first
somewhat esoteric. But time and time again throughout the Bible,
we find irrefutable evidence that God delights in allegory. From
the command of circumcision (symbolizing the covenant God
made with His chosen people) to the command of remembering
the Lord Jesus through the Communion elements (the bread symbolizing His body and the wine symbolizing His blood), we see
that God deals with His people through objects or actions in the
visible world depicting something equally real in the invisible
world.

Throughout the Scriptures, for instance, water typifies life,
sustenance, fertility, blessing and refreshing (see Psalm 23:2;
Isaiah 12:3; 32:2; 55:1; 58:11; Jeremiah 17:8). In most biblical
cases, fat—believe it or not!—represents the choicest, purest or

richest portion of something. The use of fat was an integral part of a sacrificial offering to God because of what it signified in the spiritual realm (see Leviticus 3:14–16).

With this understanding of the biblical concept of representations, let's go back to the question at hand: What significance could there be in a tree? In the Word of God, trees represent the fruit of the land. Trees are a living portrayal of the land itself, because it is through the tree that the land produces its fruit. It was through a tree that disobedience entered the land, and it was on a tree that obedience was returned to the land. "[Christ] Himself bore our sins in His own body on the tree, that we, having died to sins, might live for righteousness" (1 Peter 2:24a). Just as God used the second Adam to bridge the gap created by the first Adam between man and God, so God used a sacred tree to repair the breach between heaven and earth that came through the tree of knowledge.

This is the process of God's redemption:

> It pleased the Father that in [Christ] all the fullness should dwell, and by Him to reconcile *all* things to Himself, by Him, whether things on earth or things in heaven, having made peace through the blood of His cross.
>
> Colossians 1:19–20 (italics added)

Later we read:

> [He] wiped out the handwriting of requirements that was against us, which was contrary to us. And He has taken it out of the way, having nailed it to the cross.
>
> Colossians 2:14

God loves people *and* the land and has, in His sovereign plans, provided redemption for both.

## The Importance of "Place" in Scripture

Recently I began noticing the many, many references in the Bible to land or territories. For my own record, I decided to do a word comparison (from both Old and New Testaments) to see how the mention of land compares to the mention of other important concepts in Scripture.

Here is what I found. While the Bible mentions missions 12 times, it mentions borders and coasts 96 times. Justification by faith is cited 70 times, while countries and nations are referred to 180 times. The virgin birth appears twice, while regions are mentioned 15 times. Repentance is noted 110 times, while the earth is referenced 908 times. Baptism appears 80 times, while ground comes up 188 times. Christ's return is mentioned 318 times, while land totals 1,717 references.

Based solely on the laws of reference, can you begin to see how important land is to God?

The second generation on earth did no better than the first. Genesis 4 records the first murder in history—the slaying of Abel and the punishment exacted on Cain. When Cain slew his brother, where did Abel's blood cry out from? From the ground (see Genesis 4:10). And what did it cry out for? Justice.

As God sentenced Cain for his gruesome act, He answered the cry of Abel's blood by doing the most severe thing He could do to Cain short of killing him: He cursed Cain from the earth. I would paraphrase God's judgment this way:

> God said to Cain, "I'm going to remove from you your right to call a piece of land your own, and make you a vagabond for the rest of your life. I'm taking from you any sense of vision and goal. You will be a fugitive and will wander without a purpose."

To be a vagabond means to be homeless, and it is a curse. Moving from place to place leaves one with a desperate feeling of not belonging. Under such circumstances there can be no chance for vision or destiny to take root. Most church leaders know how true this is of some of their people. But what about the leaders themselves? In today's highly mobile society, it is tempting to pack your bags when the going gets tough and find a new town that may treat you and your abilities better. But that can be seen as a vagabond mentality, and as such it is a curse.

God is calling us to be accountable to the place where He has called us. Only when we accept that accountability can we truly see the vision and full purpose He has for our lives. In other words, a person might know what God's call is but never fully realize that potential until knowing *where* God has called him or her to do it.

## Understanding Our Assigned Sphere of Influence

Once we establish that land is important to God, we must understand that the Lord frequently sees people in terms of territory. God is a territorial God. Not that He is limited to a particular place, but He highly values certain places for certain people.

And part of how we human beings are created in God's image includes our own territoriality. This is a dimension of God's design for us. God almost always associates people and their purpose with the land. And, as we see in Jeremiah 32:41, He plants His people in a particular land:

> "Yes, I will rejoice over them to do them good, and I will assuredly plant them in this land, with all My heart and with all My soul."

Stop and think for a moment about men and women whose stories are told in the Bible. Of those who were given great visions by God, many were also asked to make a territorial commitment. Moses was directed to deliver the children of Israel out of Egypt into the Promised Land. Joshua was commanded to rid the land of giants and was given an additional territorial promise: "Every place that the sole of your foot will tread upon I have given you" (Joshua 1:3). Nehemiah was called by God to rebuild the wall around Jerusalem. Ruth vowed, in a beautiful statement of commitment, to follow Naomi to her people and be buried in the land to which Naomi would bring her.

These are only a few examples of how God has linked vision and purpose historically with commitment to a territory.

If God is indeed territorial, how literally should we take the following prayer?

> You, O LORD, are the portion of my inheritance and my cup; You maintain my lot. The lines have fallen to me in pleasant places; yes, I have a good inheritance.
>
> Psalm 16:5

According to *Strong's Concordance,* the word *lot* in this passage means destiny, portion or land fallen to a person by inheritance. When we think about the great inheritance the Lord has promised us, generally we think of it in terms of a spiritual inheritance—that is, what we have gained spiritually because of Jesus. And it is right to think this way. We will not fully grasp the true extent of our spiritual inheritance this side of heaven.

Let me suggest, however, that not all inheritance promised us by the Lord is spiritual in nature. Have you ever thought that inheritance may include a physical piece of land?

The word *lines* in this passage, according to *Strong's Concordance,* means a measuring line or portion given, again referring to inheritance. Even as God assigned a portion of land to Joshua that was to be conquered for God's people, could it be the same for pastors and leaders today? In Joshua's day giants had to be driven from the land in order for God's purposes to be fulfilled. Isn't the same still true at this hour of history? Spiritual giants—darkness, evil, corruption, anything by which the plans of Satan prevail over the plans of God—must still be driven from the land in order for the Kingdom of God to come in greater measure. And what is the greatest purpose of the Kingdom of God? *To see the lost saved!*

By this we can see that the inheritance God has for pastors and leaders today, beyond what they have gained personally through life in Christ, may include land or a community to which God has called them, in order to see His purposes fulfilled in greater measure.

If we include the meanings of *lot* and *lines,* Psalm 16:5 says that the Lord maintains our lot—the destiny, portion or land fallen to us by inheritance; and that the lines—the measuring or portion given to us by inheritance—have fallen in pleasant places. God has measured out and given to us some territory for which He will hold us responsible. Just as He gave the Promised Land to the children of Israel, so He gives us a portion of land for which we will someday answer. This part of our inheritance is also echoed in Jeremiah 32:41: "And I will assuredly *plant* them in this land" (italics added).

This does not mean every believer in Jesus Christ is guaranteed to hold the deed to a piece of property. It does mean we are placed strategically within a community or territory for the purposes of God. This is our assigned sphere of influence. Where God has planted us in the land is the place we will have the greatest impact for His Kingdom.

### An Example from Paul

Let's look at an example given by the apostle Paul. He wrote this to the church at Corinth:

> We will not boast of things without *our measure*, but according to the measure of the rule which God hath distributed to us, a measure to reach even unto you. For we stretch not ourselves beyond *our measure*, as though we reached not unto you; for we are come as far as to you also in preaching the gospel of Christ: Not boasting of things without *our measure*, that is, of other men's labors; but having hope, when your faith is increased, that we shall be enlarged by you according to our rule abundantly.
>
> 2 Corinthians 10:13–15, KJV (italics added)

The word *measure* refers to portion or limits—ultimately, our assigned sphere of influence. When Paul was relating to the

Corinthian church, he had to address opponents who had come to Corinth to undermine his apostolic authority. Yet those opponents themselves had come in without the authority of the church in Jerusalem and had leveled numerous accusations against Paul. Paul was telling them in this passage that the false apostles had tried to grow beyond their sphere of influence.

The *NIV Bible Commentary* says,

> Unlike his adversaries, Paul refuses to boast of what has occurred beyond the limits of his own ministry as the apostle to the Gentiles (Ac 9:15; Gal 2:9). In boasting about his special "field" at Corinth and appealing by implication to the existence of the Corinthian church as a vindication of his apostleship (cf. 3:2–3), he is not overstepping his limits, since historically his God-ordained field included Corinth. In fact, he had been the first to reach the Corinthians with the Gospel of Christ (v.14b; cf. 1 Co 3:6, 10).[2]

Paul used his own life to set the example. Not even he, the traveling apostle, dared go beyond his assigned sphere of influence until he had dealt with what God had given him to do in that region. Paul would go nowhere that the Lord had not sent him. R. V. G. Tasker, professor of New Testament exegesis at the University of London during the late 1950s, says of Paul in this Corinthians passage:

> It will not be *without measure* (RSV "beyond limit"). God has *distributed* (RSV "apportioned") to him a *rule*; He has marked out for him a sphere of service as a minister of the gospel, and Paul will boast only of what comes within the limit of that sphere. The word translated *rule* is interesting. . . . In this verse, it has the sense of the area measured out and allotted to Paul (so RSV "province," RSV mg. "limit"). . . . Corinth came within his rule, for he was first to preach the gospel there (see I Cor. iii. 6).[3]

This example illustrates that the Lord not only gives authority to His apostles (or pastors, prophets, teachers, evangelists), but He assigns for them a sphere, or area, in which their gift will have the greatest influence for the spreading of the Gospel.

## Deal with Your Given Portion

Even as Paul admonished the church in Corinth, we should be similarly admonished. God has given pastors and leaders the authority to do His work within an assigned place, and it is there that we will not only be most effective but find the greatest satisfaction. This is our given portion, and it is there that we are primarily responsible to do the work to which God has called us.

Here I must broach a delicate subject in the light of dealing with our sphere of influence. There is no question that we, as the Body of Christ, are to take the Gospel to every part of the world where precious souls are dying, people who have never heard the name of Jesus or who have not had a reasonable chance to hear and respond to the Gospel. But if men and women God has called as local church pastors or responsible leaders within a local church spend more time, energy and money in foreign missions work than in their own cities, something is desperately wrong.

Some believers take the mandate of the Great Commission personally, as if it is their job individually to see it fulfilled. But our Lord Jesus did not give the awesome assignment of the Great Commission to us as individuals. He gave this magnificent charge to the whole Church, the entire Body of Christ through His apostles. No one church can save the world, nor should it try.

But many churches, tragically, are sending missionaries all over the world without putting the same effort or finances into their own cities.

## First Things First

Recently I was teaching a seminar to a wonderful group of Southern Baptist pastors. When we got onto the subject of missions, a subject near and dear to the hearts of most Baptists, I did my best to tread softly. But I told them that if they as local church pastors were investing more in missions than in their own communities, I felt they were misreading the Great Commission.

At the conclusion of the teaching, the pastor running the conference (whom I will call Joe) invited me into his office. He sat me down and told me in confidence that his church was going to close in sixty days due to a lack of finances. As I had been teaching, Joe told me, he felt strongly that if he was willing to risk showing me the church books, I held the key to solving the problem.

What a statement! It was a bit intimidating to have a pastor open his church books to me and say, "Fix it!"

Still, I decided to give it a shot. First I asked Joe how much he would need per month to make it through the crisis. Joe gave me a figure. Then, as I opened the books, it did not take me long to see Joe's answer. I pointed to the missions budget and said, "There's your money. Give up your missions program for now and you can save the church."

He looked at me incredulously. I saw a multitude of questions run across his face. Finally he said, "I can't do that! What about all our missionaries out there who are counting on us?"

"In sixty days they won't be able to count on you anyway," I replied. "Wouldn't you rather make a cut now and be there for the long run?"

Joe saw the sense in what I was saying. Later that week he met with his deacons (many of whom had attended the conference) and discussed not only cutting the missions budget right away, but seeing to it, should they survive this crisis, that they poured as much money into their own community as into missions in the future.

Joe's board agreed that this seemed to be the will of God. They contacted their missionaries and explained the situation. To Joe's surprise, the majority of the missionaries appreciated the church's honesty. The board pulled back on missions and were able to save the church.

Today that church is growing again and has moved back toward investing in missions. Soon they will have a much greater missionary program than they ever had before. In addition, they are putting far more money into their local community than ever, and God has blessed them for it. That church is making more of an impact at home than it ever did when too much of their ministry money was being poured into lands that were not part of their given portion.

As Joe's experience illustrates, no church should grow prematurely beyond its designated sphere of influence. We must first deal with our given portion—which, after all, is our God-given primary responsibility. First things first.

## Would You Build on Another's Property?

Suppose for a moment that you are at a state fair. As you pass a display for a home construction company, you notice they are having a drawing for a free house. But this is no ordinary house they are offering. This house would be the home of your dreams: They would build to your specifications. Intrigued, you enter your name in the drawing. Three weeks later you are informed that you have won the grand prize! You have been given a virtual blank check to build whatever style, size and configuration of home you desire. Beveled glass, marble floors, brass fixtures—anything goes!

Here is my question: Would you take that blank check and build your dream home on someone else's property? Of course not! That would be foolish. Why? Because if you built on another's property, that home would never really be yours. You would waste the gift you had been given.

Yet such a waste illustrates an occurrence tragically common in churches today. Too often we try to build churches in communities where we have not taken spiritual possession.

The first step in taking spiritual possession of a city is committing ourselves to that community. This step, which we will look at in the next chapter, *cannot* be skipped. In much of the remainder of this book we will talk about how to take spiritual possession, once you have made your commitment. But frankly, if a pastor or leader of a local church is unwilling to make that commitment, many of these principles may be a waste of time.

The leader who continually waits for the call to a "bigger and better" pastorate is like the person who takes the gift of a home and builds it on another's property. The community will benefit very little, the gift has been wasted and the church is without a true shepherd.

By the same token, there is great power in a local church led by a pastor who has a heart for the community. This pastor will be able to say, "Hope deferred makes the heart sick, but when the desire comes, it is a tree of life" (Proverbs 13:12). And this pastor will see gifts used to their fullest and his or her hope for the community fulfilled.

# Commitment to Conquer

> We shall be judged more by what we do at home than what
> we preach abroad.
>
> John F. Kennedy

Taking spiritual possession of a territory may be a new concept to you. But wherever there are human systems and governments, the enemy has, since the fall of Adam, had a legal right to spiritual possession until he is challenged by a stronger force. Only one authority has the power to overthrow so strong an adversary: our Lord Jesus through His blood shed on Calvary.

We will see in chapters 6 and 7 why Satan has legal right to our cities, and some of the strategies God has given His people to reestablish spiritual possession. In this chapter we will look at why and how commitment to a community produces real change.

As we explore various strategies, including spiritual mapping and "smart bomb praying," it is imperative to understand that *territorial commitment can lay the groundwork for lasting change in a community.* It is like a marriage relationship, in which there is simply no substitute for commitment. If a couple chooses to live together without a marriage covenant, emptiness remains at the core of their relationship. Gratification of immediate desires with no vow of commitment ultimately leaves one or both participants longing for something more. The relationship will harbor uncertainty and unfulfilled potential until an irrevocable decision has been made, for better or worse, that binds one to the other.

In the same way, the first step in taking spiritual possession of a territory is making a commitment to that place.

## Making a Territorial Commitment

Several years ago a young man graduated from a prominent denominational seminary. Henry (not his real name) was one of the brightest and most promising students the seminary had produced, and the denomination was optimistic about his future and the important pastorate he would eventually hold.

Several months before graduating, Henry was in an intense time of prayer. As he prayed, a longing came over him for a little city of about ten thousand.

His denomination, as it turned out, had a church and parsonage in that city, but the place had been so hard on pastors and congregations that no one had ever succeeded there long term. Finally the denomination locked up both church and parsonage and vowed to send no one else to be victimized by that hardened community.

Henry knew nothing of this history. All he knew was, God had given him a burden, and it was in that city that he wanted to pastor. So he went to the denominational leaders and told them that when he graduated, he did not want to be assigned anywhere but that city.

The leaders did not want to waste the talents of this young man, who was graduating at the top of his class, on a city that could be described only as a pastor's graveyard. They had better plans for him; he could have written his own ticket anywhere. So they decided to make it tough for that obstinate young man. They offered him a prominent church in the Midwest with a healthy salary, nice staff and everything a pastor could want.

But Henry said no. He could not be disobedient to the call the Lord had laid on his heart.

Every month Henry came back and asked for a pastorate in that hard city. Every month the denomination said no. Finally, like the judge in Luke 18 troubled by the persistent widow, they grew tired of it. They gave Henry the keys to the church and parsonage and told him he had one year to make it work.

That was all he needed. He and his wife loaded up a trailer and headed to the town. When they arrived, he pulled up in front of the parsonage and unloaded the trailer. While his wife unpacked boxes, Henry unhitched the trailer and drove to the town's Little League office, where he signed up as a coach. Then, to signal his commitment to the community, he drove to the local cemetery and bought himself a plot.

Later he stood on his newly acquired plot and said, "Devil, I've come to town, and you're leaving."

A few years later Henry's was the largest church in the region. People drove in from surrounding towns to go there. And during special services, attendance in that city of ten thousand reached fifteen hundred!

Needless to say, the denomination now recognizes that commitment to a city may be the key to unlocking hard, dark communities.

## A Renter or an Owner?

Have you thought about the differences between the mentality of a renter and that of a homeowner? A renter does not look after a home the way an owner does. Generally an owner treats a home with greater care, makes the improvements and gets to know the neighbors. A renter may make only necessary repairs (and only then if the landlord pays), will seldom make permanent improvements and may not develop relationships with those living nearby. Renters have invested less so they have less to lose.

The same is true of territorial commitment. The amount we have invested correlates directly to the amount of effort we are willing to put into our communities. And our abilities and effectiveness as leaders in a local church will never reach full potential until our mentality shifts from rental to ownership. Congregations and communities know instinctively if their leaders are in it for the long haul, and they respond accordingly.

God helped His people move closer to a buyer's mentality in Jeremiah 29. In this passage a remarkable mandate was prophesied to the children of Israel, who were in bondage at the time in Babylon. But even in those extreme circumstances, the Lord called them to make a commitment and seek the peace of the city in which they were held:

> "Thus says the LORD of hosts, the God of Israel, to all who were carried away captive, whom I have caused to be carried away from Jerusalem to Babylon: 'Build houses and dwell in them; plant gardens and eat their fruit. Take wives and beget sons and daughters; and take wives for your sons and give your daughters to husbands, so that they may bear sons and daughters— that you may be increased there, and not diminished. And seek the peace of the city where I have caused you to be carried away captive, and pray to the LORD for it; for in its peace you will have peace.'"
>
> Jeremiah 29:4–7

Think about this passage in light of making your own territorial commitment. The children of Israel hardly considered Babylon their home. They longed for the day they could return to Jerusalem to get on with their lives. But God was telling them through the prophet Jeremiah to live their lives fully in the place where He had brought them. He was reminding them that He was the One who had put them there, and while they remained, they were to get on with the business of living life and blessing the land.

For us today, the application is simple. Even if there is somewhere else you long to be, ask yourself two questions:

*Who put you where you are?*
*Why are you there?*

There can be only two answers to these questions: obedience or rebellion. You are in a place either because God put you there or because you put yourself there.

Most of us, especially those in leadership, know deep in our hearts whether or not we are being obedient to God. Which of the two answers, obedience or rebellion, is true in your case?

If you are where you are out of rebellion, I have a word for you: Move, as fast as you can! Find out where God wants you and get there. Even if it feels as if you are being led out of Jerusalem into Babylon, remember that the Lord sees far beyond what you or I can see in our lives. Obedience to God always brings ultimate peace.

If you know God has placed you where you are, even if it seems like Babylon, I have a word for you: Stay there as long as God asks. Imagine in paraphrased Jeremiah 29 this dialogue with the Lord:

The Lord says, *Who placed you where you are?*
"You did, Lord."
*O.K. Now that you know I've placed you where you're living, why don't you go ahead and build yourself a house?*
"All right, Lord, I'll build a house."
*Since you're building the house, why don't you plan on living in it?*
"Sure. Why build a house unless you're going to live in it? O.K., Lord. I'll live there."
*Now that you are building a house to live in, why don't you plant a garden?*
"Plant a garden? That sounds good. I'll do it."
*Now that you're planting a garden, why don't you stay until the harvest?*
"All right. I'll stay until the harvest."
*Since you're building a house to live in, and planting a garden you will eat the fruit of, why don't you plan to get married?*
"Well, God, that's a long-term commitment. But it seems right. O.K., I'll get married."

*You are a faithful servant. Now that you have a house to live in, are enjoying the fruit of the garden you planted and have a good spouse, why don't you have some children?*

"O.K., I'll have some children."

*Now that you have a home, a garden, a spouse and some children, why don't you stay long enough to raise your grandchildren?*

"Grandchildren? Yes, Lord. It's as You say. I will stay long enough to raise my grandchildren."

*Since you are willing to build a house and dwell in it, plant a garden and eat of its fruit, marry and have children and grand-children, why don't you also seek the peace of the city in which I have placed you? By doing so, you will find your own peace.*

## Results of Territorial Commitment

There are two immediate results that take place when we commit ourselves to a local community and two long-term results. Let's look at each of these in turn.

### *Immediate Results*

In Jeremiah 29 the Lord cites two *immediate* results of making a territorial commitment.

#### THE BLESSING OF INCREASE

First we will "be increased there, and not diminished" (verse 6). Time and again, as pastors and leaders make this kind of commitment, I receive reports that they have been increased in some way—in their finances, in their numbers, in their effectiveness.

Choosing to set yourself firmly in the place where God has called you unlocks a spiritual principle that results in increase. Though I do not fully understand all the spiritual dynamics, I do know that the principle works. Over and over, when this level of commitment is made, I have seen the Lord move to stop the diminishing process and activate the increasing process. By doing so, God is showing you that you will be increased and not diminished, and that you will have everything you need to accomplish what He has called you to do.

### THE BLESSING OF PEACE

The second result of this commitment is that if you "seek the peace of the city" (verse 7), you will find your own peace. There is a spiritual peace that every city needs. Deciding to seek that peace for your community will settle something in your heart.

We know, again using the analogy of marriage, that once a commitment is made, a certain assurance settles over the relationship: You are mine, I am yours, that is that! The same is true in commitment to a community. Many pastors have told me that once they understood these principles and made such a commitment, they came to a new place of peace. Something within their hearts got settled. They knew they were there to stay, and with this knowledge came an assurance of order. Once their hearts toward their communities were established, they could get down to the business of seeing God's will for their cities come into play without being distracted by attractive pulls of the "bigger and better." You are mine, I am yours, that is that. Many of the "what-ifs" have either been answered or become irrelevant, and now the pastors can move forward peacefully within that decision.

## *Long-Term Results*

Later in Jeremiah 29 the Lord makes this beautiful declaration to His people:

> I know the thoughts that I think toward you, says the LORD, thoughts of peace and not of evil, to give you a future and a hope. Then you will call upon Me and go and pray to Me, and I will listen to you. And you will seek Me and find Me, when you search for Me with all your heart.
>
> verses 11–13

Here we see two *long-term* results of commitment. First, God's expectations for "a future and a hope" will be released on you.

What a wonderful promise! You have a future and a hope. But a future and a hope for what? What are God's expectations here?

## GOD'S VISION FOR YOUR COMMUNITY

The answer, I believe, lies in the vision God longs to pour out for your community.

Frequently I go to conferences and get to sit down with those in leadership. When I ask them what their vision is, they often reply, "We want to reach the lost, save unsaved souls, pray for the sick, touch the community." Whenever I hear this kind of answer, I immediately know they do not understand what true vision is. All these good things—reaching the lost, saving unsaved souls, praying for the sick, touching the community— are part of a *mission,* not a *vision.* They are part of the mission of every local church.

Vision, by contrast, comes in asking *how.* How will these things be done in our community? What is our plan? How does God want to use our church to further His Kingdom in this place? The answers to these questions produce vision.

Mission, the things we are supposed to accomplish, comes from Scripture and is our biblical mandate. Vision, how we plan to accomplish our mandate, comes from our relationship with the heavenly Father, who takes our personality and the personality of our community into account, gives us spiritual gifts and shows us how to accomplish the mission.

Making a commitment to a community makes a vital difference in the unseen realm. I have found in my own ministry, and that of others, that God gives a committed leader the ability to see his or her community as it really is, not as it appears to be. (This, as you recall, is the heart of spiritual mapping.) Many church leaders have written to me saying that once they settled this commitment in their hearts, they seemed to receive new eyes with which to see both the evil and the redemptive elements in their cities.

By making this commitment we gain our vision of how God wants us to affect our communities, and we see His Kingdom come in greater measure. Almost all vision, as we have seen biblically, involves a geographical or territorial commitment. And only when we make that commitment does God pour vision into us.

### A REVELATION OF GOD

The second long-term result promised in Jeremiah 29 is that God will reveal Himself to us personally (see verses 12–13). Once we have made a commitment and been given a burning vision for a place, our prayer life takes on a whole new dimension. No longer do we pray to an empty room, wishing God were there. A new sense of expectation arises in us. God promises that we will find Him; that if we are obedient and seek Him, He will come to us, speak to us and tell us what He expects.

## Unpacking Your Spiritual Bags

Wow! Even if these manifestations, both short-term and long-term, were the only results of my making a biblical commitment to a particular locale, it would be enough for me. If my relationship with the Father got closer—if I could come out of my prayer time and say I felt the Father's breath on the back of my neck, that I had been with Him and know what He expects—it would be enough for me to make a commitment to my community. And that commitment in itself would change my life radically.

But, as you will see, much, much more comes as a result of making a biblical commitment to the land.

When Susan and I moved into the Hemet area in the early 1970s, I lived and breathed for the day God would call me out of Hemet into what I thought He was *really* grooming me for. I could not wait. Hemet is known as a sleepy retirement community. It was made famous by Art Linkletter for mobile home retirement parks. People come to our community to spend their quiet, peaceful "golden years." And Hemet was located in the middle of nowhere. Civilization was somewhere beyond the closest freeway, which was eighteen miles out of town. Susan and I wanted to pastor in Los Angeles or Orange County. We dreamed of being transferred to a big church with some influence—someplace we could really be appreciated. That in no way described Hemet.

So we lived and pastored with our emotional and spiritual bags packed. Sure, we were doing what was required of us ministerially. But we were ready to leave at the drop of a hat.

### The Question

Such was my mental attitude when God interrupted me one day. I was sitting in my office at the church typing my sermon notes onto the computer. It was 2:30 in the afternoon. My door was open, people were walking through the halls and lots of normal activity was going on all around.

Suddenly something in the atmosphere of my office changed. The best way I can describe this change is to draw from the old television spy spoof "Get Smart" and its cone of silence. A bubble would drop from the ceiling, giving the parties instant privacy and silence in which they could confer on top-secret matters.

Although the cone of silence in "Get Smart" rarely worked, God's cone of silence worked very well. I did not audibly hear the voice of God. I did not see Him. I just knew I was in His presence.

As I sat at my computer, understanding that I was experiencing something of a visitation, I clearly sensed the Lord asking, *Bob, would you be willing to spend the remainder of your life in Hemet for the sake of the Gospel?*

That was the last thing I expected the Lord to ask of me! Was I willing to do such a thing? All my dreams and goals for myself and my family were wrapped up in *leaving* Hemet. Now God was asking me to *stay?*

I knew instinctively there was no right or wrong answer to the question. If I said no, God would not love me any less. If I said yes, He would not love me any more. I sensed no condemnation or pressure, just a simple question.

*May I go home and talk to my wife about it?* I asked.

After all, I thought, it would not be fair to drag Susan into this without talking it over first. In my heart, however, I knew she would say, "Absolutely not!" That would be my way out. I could go home, talk to her, she would say no, then I could say no, and I could feel free and clear in my spirit.

The Lord could see into my heart, of course. He knew all these thoughts before I even thought them. But He said, *Yes, go home and talk it over with Susan.*

I closed my office and went straight home. Susan and I went out to dinner and discussed my experience. Then we talked into the wee hours of the morning.

When all was said and done, Susan concluded, just as I had imagined, that there was no way we would do it. We would not commit the rest of our lives to Hemet, California.

But Susan and I have always made it a policy in our marriage to sleep on any big decision. We agreed to do the same in this case, even though I knew the answer by morning would be the same.

I slept well that night. My plot had worked. But when I woke up the next morning, Susan was already awake and looking at me. Since I am always the first one awake, I knew something was wrong.

"Remember what we talked about last night?" she asked.

"Ye-e-es," I said tentatively.

"It's God's choice for us, Bob," she said. "We're supposed to do it."

I sat straight up in bed.

"What?" I shouted. "Last night you were so sure! What could possibly have happened to change your mind?"

Susan replied quietly, with the wisdom of a woman, "I finally realized that if it wasn't what God wanted, He would never have asked in the first place."

I sat dumbfounded. All I could do was stare at her. Was God really asking us, despite our dreams, despite our plans, despite all we had been counting on, to stay in Hemet for the rest of our lives?

But as the truth of her comment sank in, I realized she was right. If we believed God's perfect will for us was our best course of action, we would have to let our dreams die and commit to what He was now asking us to do.

## *"Yes, Lord"*

I did not quite know how to start up the conversation with God again, so I decided to go back to where He had met with me. I went to my office that morning, sat down in my chair and said, "Lord, I have an answer for You. We need to talk."

The next moment, I sensed the Spirit of the Lord settling on me again.

"I know You know this, Lord," I went on, "but here's our answer. Yes, we will. We will commit the rest of our lives to staying in this community for the sake of the Gospel."

At that very instant, God began to reveal to me a plan for my life and for the city of Hemet. I began to write down as fast as I could what was coming to me. God was pouring understanding of what He wanted to do through me and through The Dwelling Place Church for our community of Hemet.

A real, God-given vision came to me that day. And as soon as Susan and I made the commitment to stay in Hemet, our lives seemed to click into place.

Several weeks later I shared our newfound commitment with the congregation. I explained to them that if I am caught in financial indiscretion or immorality, I cannot run. My family and I are committed to live the rest of our lives in this community with the decisions we make. We are accountable for those decisions, knowing we will not leave.

Something happened to the church, too, after we made our commitment. They seemed to settle in. They realized we were not going anyplace. Their lives had become our life.

In fact, everything around us seemed to change. Saying yes to God affected our marriage, our family, our church, our viewpoint. And our vision for the community, like a diamond, began to sparkle with new facets we had never seen before.

The hardest part of making a commitment to Hemet was setting my own dreams aside in order to fall in love with my community. It meant I had to let the dreams and plans I had for my life die. That was hard to do. But here is what I have learned about dreams we may have for ourselves. If we set our dreams aside in order to let them die, and they are not resurrected, they were not God's dreams in the first place.

Be willing to set aside whatever stands in your way of making the commitment God is calling you to. If He cannot or does not bring the dream back to you in the place where He has planted you, it was not His plan in the first place. But if you are moving in His will, He will always restore vision to you. Remember the prophecy of Jeremiah 29:11: "I know the thoughts that I think toward you, says the LORD, thoughts of peace and not of evil, to give you a future and a hope."

To this day I keep copies of the vision God poured out to me, one in my wallet and another in a safe. Every piece of that vision has either come to pass or is well on its way. God has done things in our community, our church and our family that I never imagined possible. His vision and dreams far exceeded my own.

Jeremiah 12:10–11 says:

> "Many rulers [literally, shepherds or pastors] have destroyed my vineyard, they have trodden My portion underfoot; they have made My pleasant portion [desired portion of the land] a desolate wilderness. They have made it desolate . . . because no one takes it to heart."

Let me ask you pastors to consider for a moment where you are and why you are there. Are you willing and open to listen to the Lord in this regard? Are you willing to take your community to heart? He may be speaking to you even now. Perhaps He is calling you to make just such a commitment. Or perhaps He wants to move you one more time before you commit to the land.

You do not need a personal visitation from the Lord, and a commitment may not necessarily be for the rest of your life, as it was in my case.

If you are open to hearing Him, and serious about doing what He says regarding a commitment to your community, it will be well worth it.

## Who Is God's First Choice?

Only two weeks after Susan and I committed our lives to God's work in Hemet, we had a guest minister in our church on Sunday morning. I was sitting back enjoying the message, when right in the middle of a sentence, she stopped, pointed at me and said, "God says you were not His first choice!"

A bit taken aback by the sudden prophecy, I watched her as she turned slightly away, wheeled back around, pointed at me again and said, "And God says you were not His second choice!"

*This prophecy,* I thought, *is going downhill quickly.*

I sat, silent and somewhat stunned, as she pointed her finger straight at me once again and said, "But when you said yes to God, you became His first choice."

Susan and I had shared our experience with no one, and the guest minister had no way of knowing what "yes" God referred to or what it meant in our lives. But Susan and I grabbed one another. We knew exactly what God was saying to us. He was speaking through the guest minister to say that everything necessary to complete the task He had called us to in Hemet was now fully at our disposal. The anointing, the capacity, the ability, the strength, the knowledge—everything we needed to fulfill our responsibility to the community was now available to us.

And the same is true in any community. You may not be God's first choice, but the minute you say yes, you get everything that goes with it.

The prophetic word that came through the guest minister that day caused me to consider this concept in light of Scripture. I can think of several times when God's first choice for a job did not complete the given task, so He chose another.

Take David. He was not God's first choice; Saul was. Nonetheless, David accomplished great things for God.

Or Matthias in the New Testament. He was not God's first choice, either; Judas was. Yet when Matthias was given Judas' place as apostle, he stepped into all the authority of the position as though he had been with Jesus for all three years of His ministry. As an apostle of Jesus Christ, he lacked nothing.

My favorite biblical example of God calling someone to finish someone else's job is Esther. You recall from that Old Testament book that Haman conspired to kill the Jews. But did you know Haman was a direct descendant of King Agag? Generations before, the Lord instructed King Saul to see that every one of the Amalekites was killed (see 1 Samuel 15). But when Saul defeated the Amalekites, he took their king, Agag, alive, directly disobeying God's command. Had Saul obeyed the Lord, Haman's family would have been destroyed. But Saul disobeyed God, and his job had to be finished years later by another. It was Esther, not God's first choice, who defeated Haman and ordered him and all his male offspring killed, as God had originally commanded Saul.

Who knows but that you, like Queen Esther, may have been called to your community for such a time as this? Whether you are God's first choice, second choice or last-ditch effort, when you are willing to say yes to Him and His plans for your community, you become His first and best choice!

# Part 2

# Understanding Our Enemy

# 5

# Understand Your Community

Nothing can be loved or hated unless it is first known.
Leonardo da Vinci

To understand a community, we must first understand that every city, like every individual, is unique. No two cities are exactly the same. While we may find similarities in traits, appearance, even to some extent history, the fact remains that there is no other city like your city.

God's plan for each city is also unique. Just as He created individuals with different dimensions of gifts and potential to bring about His Kingdom, so He created each city with its own divine purpose.

Satan's strategy to hold a city in bondage is also unique to every situation, and generally in direct contrast to God's plan. Here is where spiritual mapping enters the picture. It is through the methods and practices of spiritual mapping that we come to understand our communities and how best to minister to them.

## Minister to a Whole City?

The concept of ministering to a city may be new to some. We can easily picture ministering *in* a city and *to* its people. But ministering *to* a city?

Absolutely! Cities are part of God's plan for redeeming the earth. Throughout the Bible we see that cities were often a focal point for God's blessing or judgment, treated almost as if the city itself were an individual. Some classic biblical examples of cities facing God's judgment are Sodom, Gomorrah, Admah, Zeboiim, Nineveh and Babylon. In each case the city was invited, before judgment came in full force, to repent and respond to God. Each of these cities had a chance, in other words, to receive ministry.

God has also poured out great mercy on cities. The greatest biblical example of a city God loves is Jerusalem. The Bible is full of His passion for this sacred city. We read many instances in which God, using a variety of methods, ministered either directly or indirectly to Jerusalem. The prophets prophesied not only *about* the city, but *to* the city. Here is just one example of a prophet addressing the city directly: "Awake, awake! Stand up, O Jerusalem, you who have drunk at the hand of the LORD. . . . By whom will I comfort you?" (Isaiah 51:17, 19).

Throughout the Psalms we see many mentions of the glories and shame of Jerusalem. And again we see examples of someone speaking directly to the city. "If I forget you, O Jerusalem," one psalmist exclaims, "let my right hand forget its skill!" (Psalm 137:5).

Jesus also had occasion to speak directly to the city so heavily on the Father's heart:

> "O Jerusalem, Jerusalem, the one who kills the prophets and stones those who are sent to her! How often I wanted to gather your children together, as a hen gathers her brood under her wings, but you were not willing!"
>
> Luke 13:34

Not only did God send representatives to speak to the city; He sent them to minister to the physical needs of the city. Ezra was sent to rebuild the Temple, for example, and Nehemiah's mission was to rebuild the walls around the city. The Lord saw that Jerusalem was ministered to in one way or another as He saw fit. There is no doubt Jerusalem has always been a great part of God's plan.

It is true that only Jerusalem is Jerusalem. But God's love for the cities He has created is not exclusive to Jerusalem. I know beyond a doubt that God loves Hemet, California. He loves your city, too. He wants to see your community whole and healthy, with a minimum of Satan's activities that serve to blind the eyes of those who live there from the light of the Gospel.

Why are cities so important to God?

One of the best answers I have heard to this question came in a recent television interview with John Dawson, one of today's leading authorities on the role of cities in the Kingdom of God. "Cities are the greatest containers of people," he said.[1]

How true! The analogy of a container goes a long way. When we store food, for instance, the container needs to be clean and tightly sealed or else the food will spoil. Although the food itself is of primary interest to us, the container has a lot to do with whether that food will remain fresh, edible and free from unhealthy bacteria. Some attention, therefore, must be paid to the container.

I must say, at the risk of oversimplifying the issue, that this is somewhat how God views cities. People are His primary interest, which is why God sent His only Son to die. Nonetheless, the environment in which social structures develop is an important factor in how people view God and salvation through Jesus. Residents of Colorado Springs, for example, are more likely to hear and respond to the Gospel than people in Mecca, where public or private practice of any religion other than Islam is strictly prohibited.

John Dawson further explains God's interest in cities in his book *Taking Our Cities for God:*

I believe God intends the city to be a place of shelter, a place of communion and a place of personal liberation as its citizens practice a division of labor according to their own unique gifts. I believe our cities have the mark of God's sovereign purpose upon them. Our cities contain what I call a redemptive gift.[2]

## A City's True Personality

So God is interested in our cities and longs to see ministry extended to them. How, then, can we minister to a city?

Very simply, we minister to a city in the same way we minister to an individual. God deals with cities (as we have seen through biblical examples) as if they were individuals. Judgment and mercy alike fall on cities much as they do on people. And you can approach your own city as you would approach a brother or sister needing ministry. You can counsel, encourage, support—and, most importantly, pray!

As we minister to a city, it is important to take into account the city's unique personality. Each city has its own strengths, weaknesses, triumphs and traumas. We have already seen that every city, like every individual, has its own personality.

Again John Dawson helps us understand this concept:

A city is a human institution, and like all institutions it develops a creaturehood or personality that is greater than the sum of its parts. Each metropolis has unique characteristics when compared with other cities.[3]

Does the notion of a city having a personality seem strange? Some modern examples may help in our understanding. Take Las Vegas as an example. The mere mention of the name evokes a mental picture of neon lights and casinos. Las Vegas is even called "Sin City U.S.A.," referring to the many vices associated with gambling.

Another example of a city with a recognized personality is Hollywood. The so-called "entertainment capital of the world" is known for state-of-the-art films that glorify violence, sex and sins of all kinds—with the lifestyles of the filmmakers to accompany them.

New Orleans is best known for jazz music, Cajun food and Mardi Gras. These elements—particularly the indulgent, occult-based celebration of Mardi Gras—make up what and "who" New Orleans is.

Nashville is called "Music City U.S.A." and is best known for country western music (even though all kinds of music are produced and recorded there). Think cowboy hats and boots, electric guitars, recording studios, aspiring young musicians.

Each of these cities displays a definite personality. Each needs ministry. And because each city has a different history, as well as different needs, strongholds and redemptive gifts, none can be approached with a cookie-cutter method of warfare.

The same is true of your city. What personality does your city have? How did things get to be the way they are? What does Satan use in your community to keep eyes blinded or Christians complacent? What is God's plan for your city? How can it be ministered to in a way that will make a difference for the Kingdom of God?

You may know some of the answers even as you read these questions. Others will require research, prayer and discernment. Answering each question thoroughly is a crucial step in understanding your community. Then, using this understanding as a basis, we will discover in the next two chapters what gives Satan legal access to a community, and whether a whole community can be influenced demonically.

## What Is the Foundation?

When it comes to understanding your community, knowing its history is one of the most crucial elements. We cannot say we really understand a community, even if we live in it, until we have delved into its past. The history of any city is the foundation on which it has been built through the generations.

### *The Founding Fathers*

The writer of Hebrews 11:10 tells us that Abraham "waited for the city which has foundations, whose builder and maker is God." The Greek word for *foundations* in this passage means "rudimentary principles and precepts." Abraham was looking for a city whose foundations—or rudimentary principles and precepts—were based on godly principles.

*Every* city is built on rudimentary principles and precepts. The question is, which principles and precepts?

Paul used the same Greek word as the writer of Hebrews did to describe the foundation of the human personality. "According to the grace of God which was given to me," he wrote, "as a wise master builder I have laid the foundation, and another builds on it" (1 Corinthians 3:10). The human personality is formed by the way we were brought up. To a vast degree our parents, through actions or attitudes, influence many of our patterns and understandings about life.

The same is true of cities. Just as the rudimentary principles of our parents are rooted in us, so the rudimentary principles of the founders of a city—their philosophies, theories and religious dogma—are rooted in that city. The founders formed the personality of that city, the foundation on which it has been built.

If you want to know the personality of a city, go back and learn about its founders. I have yet to find an example in which the founders of a city and their attitudes about life have not significantly affected the current personality of the city.

### *Four Kings and Their Kingdoms*

In Genesis 14 we are told that Abram rescued Lot, who had been taken captive in the midst of a territorial war. In the story we are told the names of several kings and their kingdoms. Four kings situated close to one another (so the story goes) banded together to make war against four other kings, in order to expand their kingdoms. Each of the four warring kings was evil in the sight of God. In fact, the whole region later became part of Babylon, known for extreme paganism.

Each of the names of the four kings making war is significant, and carries with it some trait that was found later in Babylon.

Arioch was the king of Ellasar. *Arioch* means "vicious like a lion." Chedorlaomer was king of Elam. His name means "binder." Tidal was called "king of nations." His name means "cast out of heaven." Then there was Amraphel, the king of Shinar. We know a bit more about Shinar since it is mentioned seven times in the Old Testament. It was in Shinar that the Tower of Babel was built, and later where the Israelites were held captive for four hundred years by the Babylonians. The prophet Zechariah also saw a vision of a basket containing wickedness being moved from Israel to Shinar (see Zechariah 5:5–11). So what does King Amraphel's name mean? "Sayer of darkness."

Can you see a connection between the leaders and what happens in a city down through the generations?

These four evil kings were successful in their campaign. Two of the cities captured in the territorial war were Sodom and Gomorrah, later destroyed by God for their grave sins. It is logical to assume that these two cities had been under the rule of one, if not all, of these kings, and shaped by their character.

### *The Impact of a Godly Ruler*

Just as the historical makeup of a community can cause weaknesses within the structure of a city, so a godly foundation can bring strength. God remembers His promises to those who have been faithful to Him.

He honored David, for example, in the generations that followed that beloved king because David was a man after God's own heart. Here are two of the promises God gave David:

> "When your days are fulfilled and you rest with your fathers, I will set up your seed after you, who will come from your body,

and I will establish his kingdom. He shall build a house for My
name, and I will establish the throne of his kingdom forever."

2 Samuel 7:12–13

Not long afterward, David's son Solomon disobeyed God by
taking foreign women as wives and then worshiping their gods.
God was angry and intended to tear Solomon's kingdom apart.
But He said, "Nevertheless I will not do it in your days, for the
sake of your father David . . ." (1 Kings 11:12).

Two generations later we see David's grandson Abijam spared:

He walked in all the sins of his father, which he had done before
him; his heart was not loyal to the LORD his God, as was the heart
of his father David. Nevertheless for David's sake the LORD his
God gave him a lamp in Jerusalem, by setting up his son after him
and by establishing Jerusalem; because David did what was right
in the eyes of the LORD, and had not turned aside from anything
that He commanded him all the days of his life, except in the matter of Uriah the Hittite.

1 Kings 15:3–5

Then, 156 years after David's death, Judah was spared because
David's great-grandchildren were living in the land: "The LORD
would not destroy Judah, for the sake of his servant David, as
He promised him to give a lamp to him and his sons forever"
(2 Kings 8:19). Finally, a full 313 years later, Jerusalem was
spared once again: "For I will defend this city, to save it for My
own sake and for My servant David's sake" (2 Kings 19:34).

God honors those who follow after Him. He honors cities that
have had godly leaders for generations, even after those leaders
are gone—in David's case, at least 313 years after his death.

## What Is the Spiritual Responsibility?

Cities bear a certain responsibility in the eyes of God. Apparently they, too, like individuals, will be judged one day before
God's throne.

Jesus had strong words to say to three cities of His day. He rebuked Chorazin, Bethsaida and Capernaum for their indifference to His ministry, comparing them to the ancient cities of Tyre, Sidon and Sodom:

> "I say to you, it will be more tolerable for Tyre and Sidon in the day of judgment than for you. . . . It shall be more tolerable for the land of Sodom in the day of judgment than for you."
>
> Matthew 11:22, 24

Clearly, then, cities will face some kind of accounting in the day of judgment. They and their leaders will be held responsible before God.

I do not know if cities have souls, nor do I know how a city can be punished in eternity. Nonetheless, Jesus made an unmistakable reference to God's demand for an answer when the day of judgment comes. So I want to be assured that I can stand before the Lord on that day, having heard a territorial call to my own city, and say, "I did all that You asked of me in my city for the sake of Your Kingdom."

# 6

# Why Does Satan Have Legal Access?

If you want to have an impact, you must be committed to a collision.

In the last chapter we talked about the connection between the founders of a city and what has happened in that city down through the generations. In this chapter, in order to get more of the picture, let's take a look at how demonic forces gain legal access to cities in the first place.

## Who Is in Charge of the Earth?

Orthodox Christianity affirms that Satan is "the prince of the power of the air" (Ephesians 2:2) and "the ruler of this world" (John 14:30). The fact that Jesus and Paul were referring to Satan is undisputed. But what exactly does *the ruler of this world* or *the prince of the power of the air* mean?

Traditionally we have been taught (or have simply assumed) that Satan is the ruler of this world. It is his property and he is in control. When Adam fell, so goes this line of thinking, the earth and air became Satan's automatically, and there is no way to change this until Jesus comes back to reclaim them.

But if this is true, we have a big problem. Such an interpretation of John 14:30 suggests defeat before the battle is even waged. And this passage seems at first glance to contradict other passages like Psalm 24:1, which says, "The earth is the LORD's, and all its fullness, the world and those who dwell therein." The earth is the Lord's and all its fullness, yet Satan is the ruler of this world? Who is in control of the earth, God or Satan?

The answer, I believe, lies in the original text of each passage. In Psalm 24 the Hebrew word for *earth* is *'erets,* which connotes ground, land, earth or field. The word refers literally to *earth.* Psalm 24 is stating that the physical earth, its fruit and its inhabitants all belong to God. In the John 14 passage, on the other hand, the Greek word for *world* is *cosmos,* which refers to structures, human systems or governments. Satan is ruler of the *cosmos*—human systems and governments.

So these two passages are not contradictory at all. They are talking about two different things. The earth and its inhabitants belong to God as Creator. But since the fall of man, Satan has had the legal right to interfere with God's plans for the human race through the systems and governments we have established. Satan is the ruler of the *cosmos,* and through his control over human systems and governments, he exercises legal authority over us as human beings.

Still, it is important to realize that Satan does not possess this earth. He does not have territorial control. The earth belongs to God.

And God, sovereign over His creation, has delegated to us not absolute authority in His name, but a certain measure of authority. If we fail to act on the responsibilities He has given us—which include taking spiritual possession over our assigned sphere of influence—we will reap the consequences of this choice. Things will not go right for us (although by God's sovereignty they will always go right for Him).

Two significant events in the Bible, apart from the language of the text, lead me to conclude that Satan's legal right has to do with human systems and governments.

## Satan Gains Entrance

The first significant event—a biblical example of how Satan gains entrance through human systems and governments—appears in the book of 1 Samuel.

Samuel was a prophet of God, as you recall, sent to Israel in the days when judges settled disputes. The office of judge was set up by God after the death of Joshua to deliver the Israelites from the hand of their enemies (see Judges 2:16, 18). But Israel rebelled against the system of judges and began to demand a king to reign over her:

> Then all the elders of Israel gathered together and came to Samuel at Ramah, and said to him, "Look, you are old, and your sons do not walk in your ways. Now make us a king to judge us like all the nations."
>
> 1 Samuel 8:4–5

Samuel went to the Lord with Israel's request. God told Samuel to go back to the people and tell them the reasons they did not really want a king.

Why would God tell them they did not want a king? All the other nations had kings, and it seemed to work for them, so why not?

By having a king, Israelites would move their form of government from a *theocracy* to a *monarchy*. Under a theocracy (meaning "governed by God"), Israel's ruler was God. God's word was law. He appointed His leaders (whether prophets, priests or judges), who answered ultimately to Him. A monarchy, on the other hand, is a human system of government. Instead of God, a king would rule the land.

So Samuel went back and warned the people of all the hardships and injustices they would suffer under a king. He concluded by saying, "You will cry out in that day because of your king whom you have chosen for yourselves, and the LORD will not hear you in that day" (1 Samuel 8:18).

But why was it such a big deal? Why was God so opposed to Israel's move toward a monarchy? I believe because as the Israelites moved out from under God's rule into a human form of government, Satan could legally move in. Israel would relinquish divine protection from the full force of Adam's fall by establishing a system that was a legal base of operation for God's enemy.

Nonetheless, Israel would not listen. She insisted on a king, so God gave her one.

What a big mistake! From the point that Israel moved from a theocracy to a monarchy, the nation declined rapidly. Before that time, even though she had gotten into trouble because of rebellion, God had always gathered her faithfully back into His care. Now, however, Israel had chosen to take the government out of the hands of God. This gave Satan legal right to begin setting up strongholds—spiritual fortresses—within the government that would affect the life of every Israelite for generations to come.

Through Samuel, God had forewarned the people that they would shed bitter tears because of their new king, and that He would not help them—but not because He didn't feel like it. He was not eating sour grapes or waiting to say, "I told you so!" God loved Israel in spite of her history of many rebellions. This time, however, God was saying He *could* not help. Israel had made a choice that changed Satan's legal right within the nation. It was an invitation to the ruler of darkness.

There is one thing in all of God's creation that He will not fight: the human will. God will not override it. We cannot ask or beg Him to. He will not disregard our choices.

Perhaps the Israelites did not fully understand the gravity of the choice they were making, even though they were warned through the prophet Samuel and given a chance to change their minds. But when they said no to God, He moved back and allowed Satan his legal access. And Israel had to suffer the consequences—which resulted in bitter tears for many generations to come.

## Satan Claims Authority

One additional significant event in the Bible leads me to conclude that Satan's legal right as "the ruler of this world" has to do with human systems and governments, and that is the temptation of Jesus.

> Again, the devil took Him up on an exceedingly high mountain, and showed Him all the kingdoms of the world and their glory. And he said to Him, "All these things I will give You if You will fall down and worship me."
>
> Matthew 4:8–9

The Greek word for *kingdoms* here is *basileia,* which can also mean "realms" or "to rule." *Strong's Concordance* says this word is from the Greek root words *basileus* and *basis,* carrying the notion of the foundation of power. What Satan offered Jesus was the kingdoms of the earth, his legal right to human systems and governments—all for a moment of worship from the Son of God.

If these kingdoms were not truly Satan's to offer, the temptation would have been a mockery. Satan could not fool Jesus by offering something over which he had no authority. Furthermore, it would have been no temptation at all if it was not something Jesus really wanted. The fact is, Satan possessed these kingdoms and Jesus wanted them, which made it a legitimate temptation.

Yet Jesus chose to obey the Father's will. He did not reach out and grab Satan's bait. Instead He chose to bring salvation and redemption to the peoples of the earth in the Father's way and timing.

So I probably do not need to clarify that I am *not* suggesting in this book that we attempt a religious coup to take over the government. Some things really do need serious changing in our government, but a military takeover is not God's way, and it is not what I am advocating when I urge you to commit yourself to "conquering" for the sake of the Kingdom!

Not that am I saying to rid yourself of all political convictions, either. Be as politically active as you feel led. But it is not through politics that we will see significant ground gained for the Kingdom of God. Our battle is not against flesh and blood but against principalities and powers (see Ephesians 6:12). Only as the spiritual atmosphere over our cities changes will we see breakthroughs for the Kingdom of God.

I am advocating not political but spiritual overthrow.

## The Law of Equal Access

As Paul writes to the Ephesian church, he runs through a list of do's and don'ts for the believer. In Ephesians 4:27 he says, "[Do not] give place to the devil."

We should not give place to the devil emotionally, spiritually or any other way. But in this passage, Paul's admonition carries definite geographical connotations. The Greek word for *place* is *topos,* meaning "a locality, a literal home, a piece of land." *Topos* is the root word for *topographical.*

Why should Paul choose a geographical term in this verse? Here, borrowed from the world of real estate, is one of the best illustrations I have come across to explain how we can give *topos* to the devil.

In the United States a law dictates that no landowner can isolate or landlock any other landowner. Say you are a developer and want to build a shopping center on one hundred acres of property. Right in the middle of your land is a man who refuses to sell his single acre to you at any price. You may own 99 acres, but the law requires that you must provide that man 24-hour-per-day legal access to his one acre, even if the road cuts through your 99 acres. The following illustrates the law of equal access:

**Figure 1**

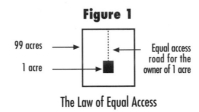

The Law of Equal Access

In spiritual matters the law of equal access works the same way. If I give up every area of darkness in my life but one, the devil still has legal access and can come and go freely. Remember what Jesus said: "If therefore the light that is in you is darkness, how great is that darkness!" (Matthew 6:23b). James 3:12 makes it clear that a fig tree cannot bear olives. But according to Jesus, darkness and light—which depict not fruit but our very wills, the actual decision-making process—can both coexist in us and have equal access.

This law has even broader applications. Think of a congregation. If individuals are holding out in darkness, can the enemy gain access? Sure he can. It might look something like this:

**Figure 2**

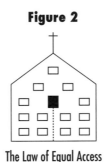

The Law of Equal Access

We all know of churches that never seem to enjoy much peace or rest. They are always having upheaval of some kind. Why is that? One possibility is that the enemy has an entryway. Someone in leadership or some unresolved issue from the past or even some satanic person stationed in the church has given the enemy equal access into that church. So Satan has the right to move in.

## It Works Both Ways

But all the news is not bad. Although we have looked at some negative examples of the law of equal access, wouldn't the same law work in reverse?

Think about your city. Does evil have a place within your community? Does it seem that the enemy has access to where you live? Once again let's apply the law of equal access. If you stake a claim in your city, *you* have equal access into the darkness. Here, using the same model, is what that illustration would look like:

**Figure 3**

The Law of Equal Access

This is one reason territorial commitment is crucial. When we come into the darkness and find one piece of soil that belongs to us, we can legally say to Satan, "This ground belongs to me and I have equal access. You cannot contest my coming or going, and I am here to bring in the Kingdom of God!"

Now that we understand how demonic forces gain legal access into cities in the first place, and before we look in Part 3 at how we can take back our cities from Satan, let's see how he gains a foothold.

# Can a Whole City Be Influenced Demonically?

> The only thing necessary for evil to triumph is for good men to do nothing.
>
> Edmund Burke

In the last chapter we looked at why Satan can gain legal access into our cities. In this chapter we will look at *how* he gains footholds that eventually become strongholds, and how he maintains these.

Here is the simple truth: Your city, which was created by God, plays a part in His overall plan for His Kingdom to come on earth. Equally true is that Satan has a plan, using whatever means he can, to pervert God's purposes for your city by keeping souls in bondage and defeat. Since Satan is a creature and not the Creator, he can be in only one place at any given time. He must, therefore, delegate the task of seeing that his corrupt schemes for your city are carried out. He does this through a hierarchy of evil spirits, full-time demonic forces assigned to your region that have committed themselves to Satan's purposes on the earth.

Noel Gibson, an Australian expert in demonology, describes it this way in his book *The Gospel Overcomes Satanic Oppression:*

> Personal activities [of evil spirits] are obviously coordinated by the higher ranking demons controlling their cities and communities, as C. S. Lewis illustrated in his *Screwtape Letters*.[1] They are the forces behind drugs, violence, lust, murder, gambling, and a host of other social evils.[2]

These higher-ranking demons, sometimes referred to as territorial spirits, have tremendous influence on the social structures within our communities. C. Peter Wagner describes high-level demonization within social structures in his book *Warfare Prayer:*

> A person who is demonized is not per se a demonic person, but rather a victim of a powerful demonic force. Likewise, social structures are not, in themselves, demonic, but they can be and often are demonized by some extremely pernicious and dominating demonic personalities, which I call territorial spirits.
>
> The view I am advocating at least permits a theology of hope. It opens up the possibility that social structures, like demonized human beings, can be delivered from demonic oppression through warfare prayer. This is why I believe that history belongs to the intercessors.[3]

Christians agree, by and large, that demonic forces are at work in the world. But we in the West have come to terms only recently with what our non-Western brothers and sisters have long known—that people today, just as in biblical times, can be demonized.

Being "demonized" does not mean the individual is demonic or possessed by the devil. It means that satanic forces are at work to keep that individual bound by behaviors, thoughts and emotional and spiritual patterns designed to interfere with the purposes of God and, ultimately, bring destruction.

The same, on a much broader scale, holds true for cities. And if we work out of the assumption that we minister to a city much the same as we minister to an individual, it is important for us to look at how the enemy torments or oppresses individuals most effectively. Here is where a basic understanding of demonology comes into play.

## Five Demonic Entry Points

The first question to ask when dealing with any case of demonization is, How did demons gain access to this person's life? Demonization does not occur randomly. No demon can attack without some kind of "legal" right. Satanic forces need a reason to force an entrance.

Those experienced in the field of demonology agree there are many entry points that may result in demonic activity. Let's look at some common entry points identified by experts in demonology, including Ed Murphy, Frank and Ida Mae Hammond, John and Paula Sandford, Charles Kraft, Noel and Phyl Gibson, John Wimber and Doris Wagner.[4] The list may not be comprehensive, but it does represent the most commonly agreed-on tactics that satanic forces use to gain entry in order to set up strongholds and bondage and bring demonic control into people's lives. One or more of these factors may be involved in any given case of demonization.

### 1. Personal Sin

An individual can easily open the door to demonic activity through personal sin—acts of either commission or omission.

Acts of commission include the works of the flesh,

> which are: adultery, fornication, uncleanness, lewdness, idolatry, sorcery, hatred, contentions, jealousies, outbursts of wrath, selfish ambitions, dissensions, heresies, envy, murders, drunkenness, revelries, and the like. . . .
>
> Galatians 5:19–21

Each of these acts of disobedience and rebellion against God leaves us with an open door to demonization. One of the most entangling and potentially demonizing of all acts of commission is sexual sin. In his *Handbook of Spiritual Warfare*, Ed Murphy states, "Demons of sexual abuse and perversion are floating in the air, so to speak, everywhere. They are among the most active, subtle, and vicious of all demons."[5]

Sins of omission can also result in demonization. One such sin that seems particularly attractive to demons is unforgiveness. Jesus warned us about this sin in the parable of the unforgiving servant. This servant, whose master forgave him a huge debt after he begged for mercy, refused to forgive a fellow servant who owed him a meager sum, but had that debtor thrown into prison. When the master discovered the servant's unforgiveness,

> "[he] was angry, and delivered him to the torturers until he should pay all that was due to him. So My heavenly Father also will do to you if each of you, from his heart, does not forgive his brother his trespasses."
>
> Matthew 18:34–35

These "torturers" are none other than demons that, through a person's unforgiveness, can torment and oppress that person until the debt is paid—in this case, until forgiveness is extended and the door to demonization is closed.

## 2. Generational Sin

What happens to a demon upon the death of a demonized person? The demon does not die with the person, so where does it go? An axiom in the text of the Ten Commandments helps us understand how God views sin in relation to generations. Exodus 20:5 and Deuteronomy 5:9 say, "I, the LORD your God, am a jealous God, visiting the iniquity of the fathers upon the children to the third and fourth generations of those who hate Me."

The shedding of Christ's blood no more changed God's mind on this passage than it changed His mind about the Ten Commandments themselves. Committing sin is much like a physical law, such as the law of gravity. Committing particular sins seems to cause a "spiritual genetic weakness" in a family, which makes its members more susceptible to that sin—and to the demonization that goes along with it. Although demonization does not occur in every case, it happens often enough that we must acknowledge it. A parent who abuses his or her child, for instance, is likely to have come from an abusive home. Drug and alcohol problems run clearly in family lines. Children, grandchildren, even great-grandchildren of an adulterer are far more likely to fall into that lifestyle than people whose families have not been tainted in that way.

Doris Wagner, who has had a personal deliverance ministry for some years, told me that some of the fiercest and most binding of all generational demons she has dealt with are those associated with Freemasonry. Doris refers to Noel and Phyl Gibson's chapter in their textbook *Evicting Demonic Intruders*,[6] which shows how Masons actually curse themselves, their families and their churches.

Though it may seem unfair, demonization can be passed from generation to generation. This cycle, unless the blood of Christ is appropriated, can go on and on. Every time the same sin is committed in a new generation, the curse of that sin is renewed for three to four more generations. The legal right for demonic activity is also renewed. Even if a generation passes that does not commit the particular sin, without the blood of Jesus to cover it, that sin remains a weakness in the bloodline.

### 3. Victimization, Rejection and Trauma

As painful and unfair as it may seem, victims of abuse, rejection or trauma are tragically vulnerable to demonization. These incidents can include rape, robbery, accidents, experiencing a tragedy or being an unwanted child. Demons can grab hold of people, especially children, through the pain of rejection, vows of "getting even," unforgiveness toward people or God, death wishes, anger, bitterness, grief or many other results of a circumstance that may be beyond the people's control.

Demons do not play fair—the younger the victim, the better. They serve a master who is out to steal, kill and destroy. These kinds of demonization cases are the main reason many with deliverance ministries feel called to see the captive set free.

## 4. Witchcraft, Occult and Fraternal Orders

Few evangelicals dispute the fact that those practicing witchcraft or occult rituals are targets for demonization. A description by Charles Kraft in his book *Defeating Dark Angels* helps us understand the many aspects of this kind of demonization:

> *Conscious invitation* of demonization is probable whenever there has been deliberate involvement with or worship of gods/powers other than the true God. Few, if any, of those involved in satanism or witchcraft escape demonization since they consciously open themselves up to invasion. Likewise, those involved in occult aspects of the New Age movement. Though such practices as seeking spirit guides and channeling are clearly demonic, not every aspect of New Age is occult. Even many of the more innocent-looking activities, however (such as those related to health and the environment), put the participants in great danger of becoming demonized. Other occult involvements to look for include organizations such as Freemasonry, Christian Science, and Scientology. Attending seances, going to fortune tellers, being involved in "table tilting" and levitation are also occult. Even more innocent-looking activities such as playing with ouija boards and tarot cards put a person in great danger.[7]

Dr. Kraft goes on to identify another form of demonization that comes as a result of these activities: when a person participates in such an activity through the invitation of someone in authority. Thus, demonization may occur when children are dedicated to spirits, gods or Satan; and when adults submit to cult leaders through dedication or satanically empowered "blessings."[8]

## 5. Cursing

Curses are more than merely wishing evil on someone. Charles Kraft defines a curse this way:

> A curse is the invocation of the power of Satan or of God to affect negatively the person or thing at which the curse is directed. The invocation may be through words or things that have been cursed or dedicated.[9]

Curses convey spiritual power, particularly if the curses are invoked by occult practices that include sacrifice, voodoo or other forms of magic.

Let me be quick to point out, however, that not every curse results in demonization. Kraft and Ed Murphy agree that demonization does not often occur solely because of a curse, particularly against a Christian. But because demonization *can* result from a curse, particularly in its strongest forms, I have chosen to include it here.

## Closing the Door

The next step in delivering an individual, once we have looked at some common entry points for demonic activity, is finding out which of these possibilities applies to his or her situation. It is important to know *why* demons are able to do what they are doing. Once we have this knowledge, we can formulate a strategy for closing the door to the demonic, rescind the legal right for demonic activity through prayer, then evict the demons from a home no longer vulnerable to their evil influence, since the blood of Jesus has been applied to the doorposts through which they once gained free access. Knowing why demons are there is the key to understanding what they are doing and how we can expel them.

There are two basic ways of knowing why demonization occurred in a given situation. First is through a word of knowledge—information given an individual supernaturally by the Holy Spirit about a situation that the individual could not have known through natural means. This is almost like spiritual intuition provided by God.

The second method of knowing why demonization occurred is through an interview with the demonized person—simply sitting down and talking with him or her. Doris Wagner asks those who come to her to fill out an extensive questionnaire many pages long, which she reviews thoroughly and prays over before a deliverance session.

## Demonic Entry Points for Your City

Now let's bring our focus back up to the city level. Similar to finding out why an individual may be demonized is finding out why evil forces are able to do what they do in your city.

First, we may learn why through words of knowledge. These will usually be given through intercessors who have committed themselves to praying for their city. Some things are so hidden that only God, according to Deuteronomy 29:29, can reveal them.

The second way to find out why evil forces are at work in a city is through "interviewing" the city. I call this getting your community to talk to you. Such interviewing is done through research. Much as Doris Wagner's questionnaire helps her understand an individual, research will help us understand our city.

To begin with, let's apply our list of demonic entry points on a citywide scale. If we are to begin researching our city, we must have some idea of what we are looking for. Simply put, *why can the enemy get away with what he does in my city?* Most of these points will be described in some detail throughout the rest of this book. But for now, here is the list:

### 1. Personal and Corporate Sin

Two kinds of sin can affect any community. The first is personal sin committed by someone with power in the city. This includes sin on a personal level (for example, sexual sin) and sin on a municipal level (for example, extortion, pandering, embezzlement, bribery, perjury, drug trafficking and murder).

The second kind of sin that affects any community is corporate sin—when one group sins against another group or directly against God. This includes activities like massacres, ethnic cleansing, slavery and broken treaties. It also includes attitudes of the heart like prejudice and racial unforgiveness. We will look more at this kind of sin and what can be done about it in the "Identificational Repentance" section of chapter 9.

## *2. Generational Sin*

Cities can also be entrapped demonically because of generational sin. This is sin that seems to plague cities generation after generation. Often the roots of generational sin go back to the founding fathers of a city or to corrupt officials long since dead. We looked at this in some detail in chapter 5.

## *3. Victimization, Rejection and Trauma*

Again we see the similarities cities have with individuals. Whole cities can be victimized, particularly in times of war. One example is the burning of Atlanta during the American Civil War.

Rejection can also be experienced on a corporate level. Usually some kind of racism, or an economic or religious issue, is involved between groups of people.

Corporate trauma can be caused by natural disasters like earthquakes, hurricanes, drought or famine. It can also be caused by political upheaval, war or rioting. Demonization can occur for the same reasons in social structures as in individuals. Corporate trauma is one of Satan's oldest methods of establishing demonic strongholds. Spiritual mapping expert George Otis, Jr., explains how it works:

> Whatever these ancient traumas might have been, they always had the effect of bringing people face-to-face with their desper-

ation. How would they resolve their challenge? . . . The overwhelming majority of peoples down through history have elected to exchange the revelation of God for a lie. Heeding the entreaties of demons, they have chosen in their desperation to enter into *quid pro quo* pacts with the spirit world. In return for a particular deity's consent to resolve their immediate traumas, they have offered up their singular and ongoing allegiance. They have collectively sold their proverbial souls.[10]

A particular people group facing some great trauma, in other words, turns to the demonic world for help, saying, "If you'll fix this problem for us, we will worship and serve you." Satanic forces are more than happy to oblige.

The price tag for this kind of supernatural intervention, however, often causes far more bondage and suffering than the original trauma would have produced.

### 4. Witchcraft, Occult and Fraternal Orders

Most, if not all, witchcraft and occult practices taking place in an organized fashion will cause demonization on some level. Witches and Satanists use their vile crafts to invoke demonic presence not only in their gatherings, but in whole cities. Rituals and rites contrary to biblical principles serve to empower evil spirits and strengthen their grasp on both individuals and territories.

Again we must include fraternal orders in which vows of allegiance, oaths of secrecy and blasphemous initiation rites are performed. Freemasonry is among the worst of these orders. J. Edward Decker, Jr., of Free the Masons Ministries quotes the following from the Freemasons' own literature:

"Man is a god in the making, and as in the mystic myths of Egypt, on the potter's wheel he is being molded. When his light shines out to lift and preserve all things, he receives the triple crown of godhead and joins the Master Masons who, in their robes of Blue and Gold, are seeking to dispel the darkness of night with the triple light of the Masonic Lodge."[11]

These kinds of beliefs serve to empower demonic activity, if for no other reason than they fly in the face of God's sovereignty and holiness by daring to place man on a par with God. This is pure idolatry—the stuff on which demons love to feed.

## 5. Cursing

Curses can be directed toward whole cities and regions and have real power over the community. Cindy Jacobs told me some years back that people involved in the occult can actually obtain catalogs of statues intended for use in cities. A person wishing to curse a city can purchase any number of statues, based on what kinds of curses they want to place on that city. What an open invitation for evil spirits to enter a territory!

## How Satan Maintains Legal Access

Once we have a basic understanding of how demonic forces gain footholds within a city or people group, we need to learn how they maintain their control. As George Otis, Jr., puts it, "How do they manage lease extensions once those people who signed the original paperwork have passed on?"[12]

There are two main ways I believe demonic forces gain these "lease extensions" in generations that follow. The first is by spiritual means, mostly through rituals and festivals. The other is by marking the territory physically.

Let's look at each of these demonic methods of maintaining control.

### Rituals and Festivals

Again I defer to George Otis, Jr., who offers this brilliant explanation as to how evil powers maintain their "tenancy rights" over the generations:

One major answer to this question is found in the authority transfers that occur during religious festivals, ceremonials and pilgrimages. That spiritual power truly is released during these activities has been testified to by numerous national believers and missionaries whom I have interviewed. Nearly all of them speak of a heightened sense of oppression, increased incidents of persecution, and on occasion, wholesale manifestations of demonic signs and wonders. . . .

It should be noted that religious festivals, ceremonials and pilgrimages are taking place somewhere in the world every week of the year. Literally thousands of these events take place, ranging from localized celebrations to regional and international affairs. . . .

These celebrations are decidedly not the benign, quaint and colorful cultural spectacles they are often made out to be. They are conscious transactions with the spirit world. They are opportunities for contemporary generations to reaffirm the choices and pacts made by their forefathers and ancestors.[13]

Such rituals and festivals may sound like something found only in the developing world, perhaps in the mystic Himalayas or in ancient Asian temples, among the lesser educated of the world. But such is not the case.

### An American Festival

Perhaps the most notable example of such a festival observed throughout the United States is Halloween, a nationwide celebration of evil. Cute costumes and fond memories of trick-or-treating lead even Christian parents to believe there is no harm in allowing their children to participate in this salute to all that is unholy. Ghosts, goblins, witches, haunted houses and horror movies are the order of the day and the surrounding season.

Intercessors have told me countless times that Halloween and the days leading up to it are without a doubt the darkest and most spiritually oppressive time of the year in the United States. Why? Because Satan is glorified openly in almost every community within the entire nation! Not exactly an even exchange for a bag of candy.

### CULTURAL SENSITIVITY OR SPIRITUAL BLINDNESS?

Another example of renewing demonic pacts comes as a result of cultural sensitivity sweeping through the United States. In one sense this sensitivity is good. God created different cultures to reflect different aspects of Himself—"redemptive gifts" we will look at in the next chapter. But along with our new regard for culture has come a tolerance for allowing what may be demonic into our society, all in the name of cultural sensitivity.

Take Native American dances and ceremonies. To the unattached bystander enjoying a family outing, these may look like intriguing expressions of the cultures of America's native peoples. But many of these centuries-old ceremonies call directly on the power of spirits and reestablish ancient pacts with demonic entities that have been worshiped in those cultures for untold generations. Open displays of animism and spirit worship are increasingly common in state fairs and community celebrations.

Festivals of demonic renewal are by no means limited to Native Americans. What about Mardi Gras or gay pride parades? Even the rites of the annual spring break for college students carry grave spiritual implications through drug use and sexual abandon. Many occult rituals, too, take place every day—rituals of which the general population is unaware.

Sadly, America is brimming with festivals and rituals in many forms that renew demonic empowerment in our communities.

### A ROMANCE OR A CURSE?

An annual pageant runs every spring in my own town of Hemet. The play, known as the Ramona Pageant, is based on a Helen Hunt Jackson novel about a romance between a Spanish woman and a Native American. The pageant itself is beautiful and acclaimed as the "official state of California outdoor play." Yet in this romantic production falls a scene in which a Native American curses the white men of the region.

Does a curse spoken in the artificial world of art and drama have any power? I believe beyond any doubt that it does. Demonic forces hardly discriminate over the particulars of an open door. The Ramona Pageant is a quaint and colorful cultural spectacle but is not spiritually benign. Six times every spring, with each and every performance, the power of this curse is renewed once again in Hemet, California.

That thought alone makes me wonder what kind of evil is unleashed continually from Hollywood.

## *Physical Markers*

My own personal map of Hemet, as I have pointed out, is peppered with red markings, each showing a location of spiritual significance. Some are spots where occult rituals have taken place. Others are religious sites or property belonging to organizations like the Church of Scientology and the Maharishi Yogi. Still others indicate places where prostitution, drugs or gang activity is rampant.

Each of these indicates a "power point"—a place where Satan has taken possession of a piece of land; a territorial marking made by the enemy to say that this land is his. Power points are Satan's markers of spiritual strongholds. The best definition of a stronghold I have heard is one I offered in chapter 2—a place that exports darkness and repels light.

Are there any areas like that in your community? Here is a series of questions designed to help you identify some possible territorial markers in your community:

Do psychics or occult stores do business in your city?
Are gangs a problem? If so, where?
Is there a red-light district in your city?
Does your city have any adult bookstores or homosexual bars?
Are there any Masonic lodges?
Are there ungodly statues or monuments in your city?

Does the artwork on the buildings display Greek gods or
   demonic faces?
Are city museums filled with sensual or demonic artwork?
Where are the witches' covens located?

Each of these sites can be considered a territorial marker.
Think of it as Satan's graffiti. Everywhere evil prevails and is
welcomed, the evil one holds a territorial marker. When we
become aware of how he marks his territory, we become more
aware of his activities within our community.

God lamented through the prophet Hosea, "My people are
destroyed for lack of knowledge" (4:6). We as Christians must
choose to open our eyes, to be aware of what is going on around
us, particularly as it pertains to the spiritual climate in our cities.

As we start looking at markers and strongholds in our own
cities, let me offer an exhortation: Don't be discouraged! Even
though we have talked quite a bit in this section about our enemy,
take heart. Knowing why your community is in bondage is a
tremendous step in winning the battle. We serve an overcoming
God who will not be defeated.

The last section of this book will help us move to the final
step—how God has equipped us as spiritual warriors destined
for victory.

# Part 3
# A Call to Victory

# 8

# Stronger than the Strongman

Even the mightiest of rivers loses its force when it is split up into streams.

In the last section we talked about how Satan gains legal access to our communities. We looked at why he can and does build powerful strongholds within our cities and neighborhoods. But does that mean we can do nothing to dismantle evil strongholds? Must the people of God merely find the most convenient way to coexist with demonic forces until the return of Christ?

Absolutely not! God has given us powerful weapons to fight the enemy. The Body of Christ, with Jesus as the Head, is much stronger than anything Satan can produce from his arsenal.

Yet even though ultimately the war is won, the battle for human souls is raging all around us. Every individual who dies without coming under the grace of Jesus Christ represents an eternal victory for our enemy and an irretrievable loss for the Kingdom of God. This is why Satan fights viciously to keep as many people as he can from the saving knowledge of Christ. It is also why God has given us powerful spiritual implements to fight the battle.

## Our Strategy

Only when we Christians recognize our God-given authority to fight the schemes of Satan can we understand that God has called and equipped us to be stronger than the "strong man" Jesus referred to:

> "When a strong man, fully armed, guards his own palace, his goods are in peace. But when a stronger than he comes upon him and overcomes him, he takes from him all his armor in which he trusted, and divides his spoils."
>
> Luke 11:21–22

Jesus, defending His casting out of demons, was talking not about armed robbery but about spiritual warfare. Where do we start? With a basic understanding of battles.

A friend of mine who is a military strategist for the Pentagon agrees that all strategists worth their salt must know three key things before engaging an enemy in battle. They are:

1. Know your own strengths and weaknesses;
2. Know your enemy's strengths and weaknesses;
3. Know your battlefield.

Many military conflicts have been lost by armies ignorant of what they needed to know before the battle began. The same is sadly true of churches or Christians who have fought principalities or powers without gathering and studying all the information necessary to meet these three criteria. Let's take the time now to understand what we need in order to be stronger than the strongman—demonic powers or agents.

## 1. Knowing Ourselves

Here is a simple truth: The way we perceive ourselves is the way the enemy will deal with us. If we see ourselves as weak, anemic and incapable of dealing with dark forces, they will treat us exactly that way. But if we see ourselves by the biblical principle that our strength is "'not by might nor by power, but by My Spirit,' says the LORD of hosts" (Zechariah 4:6), and if we recognize that intercession is our main tool, Satan has little defense. He is greatly weakened by intercession. But we must know ourselves in order to be the effective force God intends.

To know our own strengths and weaknesses, we must first be willing to deal with the truth about ourselves. Very simply put, What do you do well, and what do you not do well? Admitting the truth about yourself means putting away both pride and false humility. If you do something well, acknowledge it. If you don't do something well, own up to it. God knows what He created you for and why He created you the way He did.

We may find it easier to understand strengths and weaknesses if we break down our level of involvement in spiritual warfare to three levels. Level one involves the Body of Christ as a whole. Level two involves local churches within a particular community. Level three involves individual believers. Understanding our strengths and weaknesses on each of these levels is important because each level is different.

To illustrate these levels, let's think of a soldier in the armed forces. On the broadest level, that soldier is part of the military force of the nation, whether through the Army, Navy, Air Force, Marines or Coast Guard. On level two, that soldier is stationed on a post or base and is a member of a particular unit. On level three, that soldier carries his or her own individual responsibility within the unit. He or she is contributing to the effectiveness of the unit and, in turn, of the armed forces of the entire country.

This may help us understand how we as individual believers are placed—first in the Body of Christ (perhaps in a certain denomination); second, in a local church within a particular community; and third, as individuals with responsibilities, helping the effectiveness of the local church and, in turn, of the entire Body of Christ.

Let's look at each level of our involvement, in order to understand ourselves in the context of spiritual warfare.

### Level One: The Body of Christ

What are the strengths of the Body of Christ in battle? *Our strength is in the authority God has given us through the blood of Jesus Christ to overcome the deeds of darkness.* With Christ as our head, the war has already been won. The Body of Christ is a tremendously powerful spiritual force. In fact, on earth we are the spiritual superpower.

Perhaps the greatest weapon in our armory is prayer. Ted Haggard, pastor of New Life Church in Colorado Springs, explains why in his book *Primary Purpose*:

> When effective Christian prayer is absent, the heavens are closed and demonic/worldly influences are dominant. But when Christians start praying, the demonic influences can become so weak that a vacuum actually develops and the kingdom of God can be manifested with greater effectiveness. In these places, massive conversions, life-giving church growth, societal improvement and great spiritual encouragement occur.[1]

What's more, when we pray together in agreement, our weapon of prayer is proportionately more powerful. The Body of Christ coming together in prayer is significantly more effective than one Christian praying alone over a given situation. "The prayer of agreement," writes Cindy Jacobs in her book *Possessing the Gates of the Enemy,* "is one of the most powerful weapons that can be used in prayer."[2]

But this brings us to a major weakness Satan has taken advantage of since the days of Paul and Apollos: disunity among believers. Paul vented a bit of exasperation at the young Corinthian church for being divided over its preference of religious leaders:

> Now I plead with you, brethren, by the name of our Lord Jesus
> Christ, that you all speak the same thing, and that there be no
> divisions among you.
>
> 1 Corinthians 1:10

How much farther along are we who live on the brink of the
twenty-first century than believers in first-century Corinth? If
we judge our progress by the unity demonstrated today in the
Body of Christ, it would seem that we have not gained much
understanding in the past two thousand years!

In the same passage in Luke quoted earlier, Jesus said, "Every
kingdom divided against itself is brought to desolation, and a
house divided against a house falls" (Luke 11:17). We cannot
allow Satan to continue taking advantage of our weakness if we
hope to see great harvest in our lifetimes. I appreciate what fellow pastor Ted Haggard has to say on this subject:

> Christians embrace the same core absolutes. . . . We believe that
> Jesus Christ is the truth. He is the fact all mankind must face. We
> also believe the Bible is the written expression of the absolutes.
>
> . . . We all agree on the absolutes, but the interpretations, deduc-
> tions and subjective opinions divide us. Certainly we will have
> the interpretations, deductions and subjective opinions. But we
> make a grave mistake when we don't separate them according to
> their importance.
>
> . . . We are destroying our potential for impact on a city's spir-
> itual climate by highlighting our differences on nonessential
> issues. They unnecessarily divide us. We preach so vigorously on
> interpretations, but we sometimes fail to understand that our great-
> est strength is in the absolutes. When we believers start compar-
> ing ourselves to others on the basis of interpretations rather than
> absolutes, our influence is weakened.[3]

Disunity does not have to continue to plague the Body of
Christ. When we accept our brothers and sisters in the Lord, we
fortify our strength and dismantle our most vulnerable weakness.
Leviticus 26:8 says, "Five of you shall chase a hundred, and a

hundred of you shall put ten thousand to flight." And when we unite in agreement, all the energy we used to fight one another can be employed to fight our real enemy!

## Level Two: The Local Church

As a local pastor, I have learned two major lessons with regard to strengths and weaknesses. I offer them here as admonitions. First, figure out what you are good at and do it. Second, figure out what you are not good at and stop doing it.

It is that simple, yet it took me years to learn. It was hard for me to admit there are some things other churches do well that our church simply cannot do. Here is what I used to do. I would watch a church on the other side of town start a new program that resulted in great church growth. *If they can do it,* I would think to myself, *we can do it just as well, if not a little better!* Then I would go to my board with great excitement and say, "The church across town has a new program. It seems to be working. I think we can do the same thing. Let's try it." So we would try it. But more often than not, the program would fail miserably.

What a disappointment! I ended up with a whole cemetery of dead church programs that somehow I had managed to slaughter.

Through many hard experiences, I found out there are some things The Dwelling Place in Hemet, California, is simply not good at. But those are not the things God expects from us. By the same token, I learned that we are greatly gifted in certain areas. The things that come naturally to us are the things we need to concentrate on.

In the past few years the pastors of Hemet have enjoyed unity and mutual support as we have learned to view one another as brothers and sisters rather than competitors. (But such has not always been the case; more about this in chapter 10.) As we have come together, God has shown us an amazing thing: Every church in our community has a unique strength that adds to the richness of the Christian community in Hemet.

God has given us just what we need. Some churches have great expository preaching while others have exceptional Sunday school programs. Some excel in evangelism while others focus on social needs. Some minister to the retired community while others reach gang members. Some feature exciting contemporary worship while others have beautiful pipe organs and majestic choirs.

Each church has its own strengths and contributes uniquely to the work of God in our valley. Together, we have discovered, we form a beautiful picture of the Bride of Christ in our community.

### Level Three: The Individual

A plethora of information available in Christendom today helps us grasp our strengths and weaknesses as individuals. It is vital for us, as we think about spiritual warfare, to understand our personal spiritual gifts.[4]

Every member of the Body of Christ has been given one or more spiritual gifts. Each is important in (among other things) spiritual warfare. Remember, spiritual warfare in our communities is essentially seeing Satan's dominion diminish and the Kingdom of God come in greater measure. *Every* Christian has a part to play in accomplishing this task. Those with gifts like mercy, hospitality, helps and administration are just as necessary as those with gifts of pastoring, interceding and ministering deliverance.

The individual believer needs to know (just as the local church does) how he or she is gifted, and then key in on those areas. If each of us would do that, our effectiveness as a Body would increase greatly.

## 2. Knowing Our Enemy

We looked in some detail in Part 2 of this book at why and how Satan gains and maintains strongholds within our communities. So we will not spend much more time on it here, other than to point out one major strength Satan has in the Western world today: the ignorance of the Body of Christ.

By and large we have not really understood why or how Satan gains inroads into our communities. In this decade, however, much light has been shed on our enemy's secrets. This leads us to understand his greatest weakness: *his battle plans exposed.* The more we understand about our enemy and his kingdom, the weaker he gets.

We spend time studying and learning about his ways not in order to glorify him, but in order to learn how he can best be defeated.

## 3. Knowing Our Battlefield

Now we come to the heart of spiritual mapping: knowing our battlefield—in this case, our city.

No general would take troops into an unresearched area to wage war. Nor should we in spiritual warfare. Knowing ourselves and our enemy is not enough. If we do not know our battlefield, we will get into a lot of trouble. If we do not understand our community, we will not wage war effectively.

### *The Tragedy of Antietam*

The Civil War Battle of Antietam clearly illustrates the need to know a battlefield before the battle begins.

In September 1862 the Union Army was attempting to penetrate Confederate territory by invading the town of Sharpsburg in northern Maryland. The Union troops, under the command of Major Ambrose Burnside, would have to cross the Antietam Creek. Major Burnside decided that, in order to gain access to Sharpsburg, he must gain control of a certain bridge that crossed the creek.

The Confederate Army had only a small contingent of troops guarding the bridge when the attack began. Nonetheless, as the Union soldiers attempted to cross the bridge, the Confederates were able to stay them off by the thousands. The Union Army suffered 22,000 casualties in one day attempting to cross that bridge over the Antietam Creek.

But if Burnside had taken the time to research the land, he would have discovered that less than a mile downstream, the creek was shallow enough for his troops to walk across. The bridge was not really necessary for launching his offensive. In September 1862, the Union Army suffered 22,000 casualties for nothing more than a lack of research.

Major Burnside's mistake is a great lesson for us today. Nothing can take the place of good research that will help us understand our battlefield.

### The Unobvious May Be a Key

The key to our battlefields in spiritual warfare may not always be as obvious as local topography should have been to Major Burnside. Satan will often hide things right in front of us, veiled in a way we may not expect.

We have looked in the obvious places, for instance, for the enemy's works—places like red-light districts, slums, casinos and bars. There is no question demonic strongholds are firmly in place where we find these establishments. Very often, however, they are not where the heart of a stronghold is.

Satan uses vice and poverty (among other things) to keep vast groups of people in tremendous bondage. He also uses the greed of a few wealthy people to his best advantage. As a result, prostitution and drugs may be a problem in one section of town, while the people supplying those services (as well as the demons behind them) live and operate in another part of town. It is often in the clean, quiet, well-tended places that demonic forces are hardest at work, using people with power and influence to keep communities bound.

### A Story of the Unobvious

When Nikita Khrushchev was appointed first secretary of the Communist Party in 1953, the Soviet Union had major economic problems. Among the contributing factors was a problem with factory workers throughout the U.S.S.R. They were stealing from factories at such a rate that the pilfering was contributing to the destruction of an already shaky economic base.

Khrushchev had to do something. He decided to tighten security at all the factories throughout the nation. He had each factory secured with barbed wire so employees could exit only through the main gates. Then he put checkpoints at the gates to be manned by government troops, whose job it was to check all employees to make sure they were not taking anything they should not.

The true story goes that in one town lived two men, Joe and Ivan (as we will call them). They had grown up together and were best friends. Ivan became a factory worker in the local sawmill and Joe became a soldier. It happened that Joe was assigned to guard the gate at the factory where Ivan worked.

One night as Joe was guarding, Ivan came up to the gate to go home, pushing a wheelbarrow with a huge bag tied at the top. Joe stopped him and asked what was in the bag. The bag was full of wood chips, Ivan replied, which employees were allowed to take home. But Joe was duty-bound to check it out. He dumped out the whole bag and found nothing but wood chips. He shoveled all the wood chips back into the bag and Ivan went home.

For more than a week the same thing happened. Every evening Ivan wheeled up a huge bag and Joe dumped it out to check, only to find wood chips.

Joe knew his friend very well. Something more was going on, he realized, but he could not figure it out. Finally, on the tenth night, Joe said to Ivan, "I'll make you a deal. I know you're stealing something and *you* know you're stealing something. If you'll tell me what you're taking, I won't report you."

After Joe gave Ivan his word that he would not get into trouble, Ivan told him, "Joe, I'm stealing wheelbarrows!"

Because Joe had been focusing on the bags, he did not see Ivan taking the wheelbarrows right out from under his nose, stealing what lay in plain sight.

That is often how things happen in our communities. We cannot see what is really happening in certain situations because we are too focused on the obvious.

## *A Hunter's Lesson*

God used one of my own hobbies, deer hunting, to illustrate this principle to me. (Let me say at the outset that I know some people have a problem with hunting. But I grew up hunting with my dad, whose family back in Kentucky lived on what they hunted.)

Years ago I was exploring a secluded canyon, scouting for the upcoming deer season. I hiked over a ridge and looked down into a huge basin full of oak trees, sagebrush and a running stream. There in the canyon I saw the biggest California buck deer I have ever seen! As I looked at his tracks, I noticed he had a particular cleft right front hoof. Because of that hoof, I knew I would be able to track him when deer season came.

When the season arrived, I hiked back into the canyon. Sure enough, there were the telltale tracks of the buck; but try as I might, I could not find him. The following year the same thing happened.

For years I hunted for my prey. I would find fresh tracks and know he had been there not a half hour ahead of me. That buck had to be right around the area, but he always seemed to elude me.

One very hot day I was sitting by the stream next to more fresh tracks from my quarry. I was frustrated. Hunting that buck was reminding me of how ineffective our church had been in Hemet. At this time we were still doing our scud missile praying and everything we knew how to do, but had seen little change in our city. My frustration at both situations seemed to come to a head.

*Lord,* I prayed, *I'm dealing with darkness in our community in the same way I'm hunting this deer. I feel I'm always one step behind and I can never catch up!*

At that moment I sensed the Lord saying, *Look in the un-obvious.*

I sat there for a moment, then shook my head, got up and started walking out of the canyon. Surely God was not helping me hunt deer!

But as I climbed to the top of the canyon, I heard the Lord on the crest of the hill. *I said, look in the unobvious.*

I stopped in my tracks, turned and looked into the valley. Across the canyon I spotted a broad, sprawling oak tree about ten feet tall growing on the steep hill amidst some craggy rocks. I could not remember having seen that tree before. And in the shade of that old oak tree stood the buck, looking straight at me.

As my quarry and I stared at each other, I felt the Lord say, *That's how you've been looking for Satan. You've been looking in the watery places and in the wooded canyons—all the places you thought you'd find him. But all the while he has been look-ing at you, watching from right under your nose and getting away with it. Now look for darkness in every single area of Hemet.*

I learned a great lesson that day. No area in a community is *not* fair game for our spiritual enemy. Every level of life is sub-ject to scrutiny in intercession. We must know our battlefield. As we intercede, God will reveal to us the strongholds behind the darkness in our cities. Satan knows full well that he cannot con-tinue to hide or steal from under the  very noses of a praying and discerning church. Sooner or later he will be discovered and his stratagems exposed.

## Awaiting Redemption

As you make a commitment to see your community as it really is, you will begin to notice how the enemy has worked for evil in the city you love. You may see how the occult func-tions in your community as you have never seen it before. You may find out what is really going on with the leaders in the com-munity and begin to understand their hidden agendas. It is not unusual for righteous anger to rise up in you. But even as you gain understanding, exercise caution. Fight the urge to charge into a blazing hell armed only with a water pistol.

As we find areas of darkness in our community and identify strongholds, we must move slowly and be covered in prayer. God wants to show us aspects of our community that will require wisdom and discretion. But we need to know how to keep His secrets and fight our battles in prayer. Proverbs 10:14 (TLB) says, "A wise man holds his tongue. Only a fool blurts out everything he knows; that only leads to sorrow and trouble."

God has created cities (as I mentioned earlier) to play a part in His overall plan for the earth. Knowing our battlefield does not mean only knowing why, where and how evil plays a part in our community. It also means knowing why God created our particular city and what He wants accomplished.

A key to understanding why God created your particular community comes in knowing your city's "redemptive gift"—its personality and talents that enable it to carry out God's intention. John Dawson has led the way in helping us understand the concept of the redemptive gifts of a city in his book *Taking Our Cities for God:*

> I believe God intends the city to be a place of shelter, a place of communion and a place of personal liberation as its citizens practice a division of labor according to their own unique gifts. I believe our cities have the mark of God's sovereign purpose upon them. Our cities contain what I call a redemptive gift.
>
> What message would an angel of the Lord bring concerning your city? Would God reveal a divine purpose? On the other hand, Satan will do anything in his power to accuse your city, to malign its redemptive gift.
>
> Let me give you an example. A citizen of Amsterdam has a right to be proud of the centuries-old tradition of hospitality and tolerance that mark the culture of that city. Amsterdam is a genuine city of refuge, like world-famous Geneva or some of the cities of the Levites listed in the Old Testament.
>
> Today, however, it's a city known for tolerating open drug sales and legal prostitution. This is plainly a perversion of a

gift. Amsterdam needs a fresh picture of itself functioning in righteousness, an identity rooted in the prophetic vision of its Christian community. Indeed God has begun to raise up dynamic ministries in this, one of Europe's darkest cities.

Determining your city's redemptive gift is even more important than discerning the nature of evil principalities. Principalities rule through perverting the gift of a city in the same way an individual's gift is turned to the enemy's use through sin.[5]

So face the happy challenge of discovering the redemptive gift of your city—and then work with God to help fulfill that gift. Jack Hayford summed up in a poem our call to seeing redemption come to our cities:

> Something is happening among God's people.
> With cities and towns,
> It's happening right now.
> Two kingdoms are wrestling for the city's soul.
> It isn't too late to win,
> if we will rise up early.
> Cities deserve a tomorrow, too.
> They're unable to possess it for themselves.
> All children of Joshua—arise![6]

# 9

# A Call to Repentance

Remorse is impotence. It will sin again. Only repentance
is strong; it can end anything.

Helen Miller

This is, without a doubt, the most exciting time in all of history to be a Christian! The Spirit of God is at work in His Church in unique ways. Few of our grandparents could have predicted the kinds of activity in which we would be involved. This book, for example (as well as many others I have mentioned), could not have been written even 25 years ago. God has been maturing the Church to become a warrior in the late twentieth century for His Kingdom.

Because of the times in which we find ourselves, it is vital—perhaps now more than ever—to be sensitive to the Holy Spirit's leading. Revelation 3:22 says, "He who has an ear, let him hear what the Spirit says to the churches." Many Christian leaders agree that the Spirit is leading the Church today into a season of repentance. This call to repentance is both conventional and unconventional.

It is conventional in that we must seek God's forgiveness for personal sin as well as for sin committed by the Church. Without asking His forgiveness, we have no business attempting any kind of spiritual warfare. But the call to repentance is unconventional in that the object of repentance includes much more than the sins for which we as individuals are responsible.

The term given to this broader expression of penitence is *identificational repentance*—an act by which we identify with and ask forgiveness for the sins of a group (a city, for example, or a nation) with which we are connected. Identificational repentance is a powerful weapon in our arsenal of warfare whose time has come.

Cindy Jacobs, one of today's leading experts and practitioners in the area of identificational repentance, has helped facilitate this response to the call of God all over the United States and in many nations of the world. I am grateful to Cindy for being the pioneer in this teaching over the past decade, and as it appeared in an article in *Releasing Destiny: A Spiritual Warfare Manual for Nashville and Country Music* (Daniel 1 School of Leadership, 1993).[1]

## The Principle of Remitting Sins

The remitting of sins (*remit* is the King James word for *pardon* or *forgive*) has not been widely taught or understood in the past. Now, however, we are coming to understand that it is a vital part of spiritual warfare. Jesus Himself told us that we have power to "remit" or forgive sins: "Whosoever sins ye remit, they are remitted unto them; and whosoever sins ye retain, they are retained" (John 20:23, KJV). The ramifications of our forgiving or not forgiving, in other words, are significant.

Later Jesus modeled the principle of remitting sins on the cross when He said, "Father, forgive them, for they do not know what they do" (Luke 23:34).

Remitting sins is actually a form of binding and loosing. Recall Jesus' words to His disciples: "Whatever you bind on earth will be bound in heaven, and whatever you loose on earth will be loosed in heaven" (Matthew 18:18).

When a person holds unforgiveness toward someone else, it not only binds the unforgiving person in his or her own heart, but it binds the one who committed the sin. Why is that? Because, as we saw in John 20:23, the sins of whomever we forgive are forgiven him or her, while the sins of whomever we do not forgive are "retained." Satan has a legal right to establish a stronghold in the midst of a situation in which forgiveness has not been extended. When forgiveness flows, on the other hand, it looses both the perpetrator and the victim from Satan's grasp.

This does not mean, of course, that the one who committed the sin is not accountable before God for what he or she has done. Each person needs to come before the throne of grace and ask God's forgiveness. But when he or she has been forgiven by the other person, Satan's legal right is gone and the Lord can begin to move in on the situation, bringing conviction, forgiveness and healing.

· This is why Jesus asked the Father to forgive those who hung Him on the cross. He loved them so much that, even as He suffered unimaginable anguish at the hands of the bloodthirsty mob, He longed to see God move on His people and help them see the Messiah their hearts yearned for. But without the extension of forgiveness, Jesus knew their blinders could never fall.

## Can Cities and Nations Sin?

So, what does the principle of remitting sins have to do with cities, people groups and nations? Everything!

Because the United States prizes individuality, it is natural for Americans to grasp principles on an individual level. But our lack of teaching about cities, people groups and nations as corporate units has left us unable to see that God holds cities and nations accountable for sin, and that individuals are held responsible for sins committed within their own groups.

A good example of this is Sodom and Gomorrah. Have you ever thought about the children who lived there? Had they committed the sins for which those cities were destroyed? Probably not. Yet they, along with the adults, were held accountable in judgment. Why? We get a clue from Exodus 20:5 and Deuteronomy 5:9—accounts of the Ten Commandments we looked at in chapter 7 that help us understand how God views sin in relation to generations:

> "I, the LORD your God, am a jealous God, visiting the iniquity of the fathers upon the children to the third and fourth generations of those who hate Me."

Even the little ones, harsh as it may seem, are held responsible for corporate sin in the form of iniquity. It is the principle of sowing and reaping. Let's say a pregnant woman uses drugs and her baby is born with a deformity. Is the baby guilty of taking the drugs? No. But unless the Lord intervenes with His healing power, the child will carry that deformity (or "iniquity") the rest of his or her life.

And in the matter of corporate sin, the iniquity is passed on to the third and fourth generations.

### *Another Biblical Example*

It is important to recognize that whole people groups can sin, not only against God but against other people groups. Such corporate sins have caused great division and even cursing between people groups, just as sins cause division and cursing between individuals. And the sins of a nation can cause God to withhold His blessing, as He did in the case of Israel and the Gibeonites:

> Now there was a famine in the days of David for three years, year after year; and David inquired of the LORD. And the LORD answered, "It is because of Saul and his bloodthirsty house, because he killed the Gibeonites."
>
> 2 Samuel 21:1

This passage raises several interesting questions:

1. *Who were the Gibeonites?* The Gibeonites, as we learn from Joshua 9, were a group of people who, generations

prior to Saul's reign, tricked Joshua into making a treaty with them, guaranteeing their safety.

2. *What did Saul do?* We read in 2 Samuel 21 that Saul killed some of the Gibeonites and devised a massacre of the rest, thus breaking Israel's treaty.

3. *Why did God bring famine to the land as a result, since the Gibeonites had deceived the Israelites into the covenant in the first place?* God takes treaties and covenants seriously. Even though Joshua had been tricked, God held his descendants responsible for honoring the covenant with the Gibeonites. Generations later, when Saul broke the covenant, God removed His blessing from the land.

4. *Why did David have to repent for Saul's sin?* Exodus 20:5 says that iniquity is visited "to the third and fourth generations." David knew this principle, and knew he had to deal with the cursing Saul had brought on his people by sinning against the Gibeonites.

5. *What had to be done in order to "cleanse the land"?* Second Samuel 21 goes on to tell us that seven of Saul's descendants had to be hung (or crucified) "before the LORD" (verse 6). Had those seven descendants been responsible for the breaking of the covenant? No. But it is important to remember that "without shedding of blood there is no remission" (Hebrews 9:22).

What a sobering story of how seriously God treats sin between nations!

## How Is Such Sin Remitted?

Have any treaties been broken in your nation or city? What about with Native Americans? History tells us that more than 350 treaties have been broken. Agreements are still violated today. What does God think of that? How can Christians expect Native Americans to come to the Lord while there is still unremitted sin? No wonder these wounded peoples are so resistant to the Gospel!

What about the Japanese-Americans who, during World War II, were forced to give up their homes and live in detention centers while their sons were shipped off to war? What about the Chinese people who built our railroad system as virtual slaves, many dying or being killed because the railroad companies did not want to send them home? How about the disgrace of slavery and the way African-Americans have been treated in this nation, even after the Emancipation Proclamation, even today?

These are some of the sins for which Americans carry corporate guilt. Because we live after Jesus' death and resurrection, we have available to us His blood that was shed for the remission of sin. Through intercessory prayer we can ask God to forgive not only our sins, but the sins of our people.

That is what Daniel asked. Listen to his confession and request on behalf of his people Israel:

> "We have sinned and committed iniquity, we have done wickedly and rebelled, even by departing from Your precepts and Your judgments. . . . O Lord, to us belongs shame of face, to our kings, our princes, and our fathers, because we have sinned against You. . . . O Lord, hear! O Lord, forgive! O Lord, listen and act! . . ."
>
> Daniel 9:5, 8, 19

Had Daniel himself rebelled and departed from God's precepts? This young man, with the heart of an intercessor, came apart before God three times a day (see Daniel 6:10) and was told by the angel Gabriel that he was "greatly beloved" (10:11). No, Daniel was identifying with the nation of Israel and asking God for forgiveness on her behalf.

The blood of Jesus has the power to cover even the corporate sins of a nation. In fact, only Jesus' blood can wash those sins clean and heal the deep wounds that plague a society. Those sins must be remitted. We must learn how to identify with our people, as Daniel did, and ask God's forgiveness, whether on behalf of our country or our local community.

This is the heart of identificational repentance—a powerful tool in the hands of the Church because it removes Satan's right to blind victimized peoples to the Gospel of Jesus Christ.

## Is Identificational Repentance Biblical?

So far in our brief study, we have looked at passages from both Old and New Testaments. Is it a problem that much of the theology and practice of identificational repentance comes from the Old Testament? Not at all! Old Testament passages—including the examples of Ezekiel (see Ezekiel 4) and Nehemiah (see Nehemiah 1:6–10)—are as valid in substantiating the practice of identificational repentance as anything we find in the New Testament. Dr. Gary Greig, associate professor of Old Testament at Regent University, explains why:

> The Old Testament was the Bible of the New Testament Church. F. F. Bruce, the well-known evangelical, British New Testament scholar, pointed out in his study of Old and New Testament canons and manuscripts that the Old Testament was the only Bible the early Church had before the New Testament documents began to be collected in the late first century A.D., some thirty or more years after the early Church pictured in the Book of Acts:
>
> The Old Testament was the Bible of our Lord and His apostles, and its authority was fully acknowledged by them. . . .
>
> The Old and New Testaments, in fact, cannot be dissociated.
>
> . . . We cannot understand the New apart from the Old. The Old Testament is to the New as the root is to the fruit. It is a grave mistake to think that the fruit of the Spirit in Christianity will grow and ripen better if the plant is severed from its roots in the Old Covenant.[2]
>
> Since the Old Testament was the Bible of the New Testament Church, we need to ask what the Old Testament has to say about sin and confession in general, and generational sin, identificational repentance, and corporate confession in particular.[3]

So is identificational repentance biblical? Yes! It is not explained in the New Testament for the same reason that the Ten Commandments are not reiterated. The New Testament Church, as Dr. Greig points out, had the Old Testament as its Bible. New Testament writings in no way contradicted or replaced the Old Testament. The epistles, for instance, were written to address contemporary issues and give additional instructions to first-century believers as the need arose. Yet all the while the Old Testament stood (and stands) as the Word of God.

As we talk about instances of identificational repentance, therefore, we must recognize that men and women of God were setting examples for righteous and biblical repentance that would remain valid into the twentieth century and beyond.

## A Legacy of Violence Is Broken

In 1990 God placed a special burden of intercession on The Dwelling Place for the Soboba Indians. For many years their reservation had suffered a disproportionate amount of violence. During the 1980s it was rated by the U.S. government as one of the most violent reservations in the country, with an average of one murder per month. In fact, its reputation kept many county officials and social workers from coming onto the reservation at all. Even ambulance drivers and firefighters would not enter without a police escort.

As we undertook spiritual mapping, we learned the history of a canyon located in our valley. This canyon was the site of a massacre about 350 years ago in which hundreds of Soboba women, children and elderly men were slaughtered.

Further research told us that the Pachanga tribe, while in a state of drought, had sought to plunder their Soboba neighbors (then called the Eva tribe) thirty miles to the north. The Pachanga, in a surprise raid, killed the Soboba men while they were working in their fields. Then they pursued the women, children and elderly men into a nearby canyon, where they slaughtered them as they pleaded for their lives. To this day the site is called Massacre Canyon.

After we discovered these facts about Massacre Canyon, we began to ask ourselves if the shedding of innocent blood some 350 years ago could have any bearing on the current legacy of violence on the Soboba reservation. As we prayed, we sensed not only that this atrocity had indeed defiled the land—God told the Israelites in Numbers 35:33, for example, that atonement *for the land* needs to be made when bloodshed has taken place—but that this event had become a legal entry point for a spirit of violence on the Soboba reservation.

So we called for a solemn assembly—a prayer meeting in which sins are remitted—to be held in Massacre Canyon. Our assembly included born-again representatives of both the Pachanga and the Soboba tribes. Both Native Americans were women in their mid-forties, intercessors who prayed for revival on their reservations. We also invited key intercessors who understood the purpose of a solemn assembly.

One Saturday afternoon in the summer of 1990, about a dozen of us, including my wife, Susan, drove up to the head of the canyon and hiked to the approximate location of the massacre. After a time of prayer, things just started to happen. The Pachanga representative dropped to her knees in front of the Soboba representative and began to weep.

"Please forgive us for massacring your helpless people," she said. "I ask forgiveness for the sins of my ancestors. Would you forgive us for the suffering we caused you?"

"I extend forgiveness on behalf of my people," said the Soboba woman, "in the name of Jesus. I release the Pachanga people from the sin of the massacre. And Lord, I ask that You bless the Pachanga people."

Then the Soboba woman began to cry and crumpled onto the ground in front of the Pachanga woman. "Would you, in turn, forgive us for the hatred and cursing that my people have leveled against yours? Will you forgive us for our bitterness toward your people, and release us from that bitterness?"

"I offer forgiveness on behalf of my people," said the Pachanga woman, "and do release your people from your bitterness."

Both women, still weeping, embraced one another as the rest of us (scarcely dry-eyed ourselves!) stood in a circle around them.

I handed each person in the group the elements of Communion, the bread and the cup representing the redemptive work of Jesus Christ that now covered the sin committed here. Once we had received the elements, I took the remainder of the cup, representing the blood of Jesus, and poured it onto the ground to symbolize His atonement for the innocent human blood that had been shed violently on this land. Then, based on the repentance and forgiveness that had taken place, we bound a spirit of violence in the mighty name of Jesus and commanded it to loose the Soboba people from its murderous acts. And finally we drove a three-foot wooden stake into the ground as a prophetic act of redemption— a physical gesture or posture or act portraying the Lord's redemptive will and purpose.

Scriptural examples of prophetic acts abound. Jeremiah told Seraiah to tie a stone to a book of prophecies against Babylon and cast it into the Euphrates River, announcing God's intention to sink that empire (see Jeremiah 51:60–64). The prophet Ezekiel was instructed to lie on his left side for 390 days, one day for each of the years of the sins of the house of Israel, and then on his right side for forty days, one day for each of the years of the sins of the house of Judah (see Ezekiel 4:4–6). In this way the Lord portrayed dramatically the iniquity of His people.

After our Communion service in the canyon, Susan felt the Lord prompting her to suggest that each of us pick up a grapefruit-sized stone and build a memorial in some spot on the Soboba reservation (located about two miles east) as a mark of God's redemptive work. The significance of the memorial would be like that of the one built by Joshua and the Israelites after the Ark of the Covenant crossed the Jordan riverbed, on dry ground, into the Promised Land:

". . . Each one of you take up a stone on his shoulder . . . that this may be a sign among you when your children ask in time to come, saying, 'What do these stones mean to you?' Then you shall answer them that the waters of the Jordan were cut off before the ark of the covenant of the LORD; when it crossed over the Jordan, the waters of the Jordan were cut off. And these stones shall be for a memorial to the children of Israel forever."

Joshua 4:5–7

As we hiked out of the canyon, our Soboba sister suggested that, since we needed a site on the reservation of legitimate spiritual authority, we build our memorial on the grave of her grandmother. This woman, she told us, had been a believer and intercessor for the reservation.

So we located the grave and drove a second stake into the ground next to the headstone—another prophetic redemptive act connecting the massacre and the reservation. Around the stake we built our memorial with the stones we had carried. And once again we asserted our biblical authority, in the name of Jesus, over the spirit of violence that had taken so many lives of the Soboba people.

Since that summer day in 1990, there has not been a single inner-tribal murder, in spite of the past reputation of violence on the reservation—a reputation that no longer exists.

## How Is Identificational Repentance Carried Out?

Cindy Jacobs, in her article in *Releasing Destiny: A Spiritual Warfare Manual,* enumerates the steps of identificational repentance.[4]

First, she says, it is vital to have good, solid research. Find out about the first inhabitants of your area and what happened to them. Were any treaties broken? Has there been any sin between people groups? How were African-Americans treated? What about other groups of immigrants? As these kinds of questions are asked and answered, the sins and traumas of the people generally become apparent.

The next step is to plan and hold an interdenominational "solemn assembly" prayer meeting in which sins are actually remitted. Here is a model of how to go about it:

1. First, have a "council of war" with all the pastors who are willing to attend, since they are the spiritual gatekeepers of the city. It is important for them to be in agreement and understand what the goals of the meeting are.
2. Appoint a leader who understands the strategy. A minister called to strategic-level intercession is critical at this point. The Lord often gives special discernment to this person to set the pattern for the meeting.
3. Let this leader act as a facilitator. The leader may or may not do the actual repenting. His or her role is to see that those at the assembly understand what is going on and help guide whoever is doing the actual repenting and forgiving.
4. Have the local ministers, the spiritual gatekeepers of the city, pray and repent of each of the sins and iniquities of the city. Also, as they repent to one another for splits and schisms in the Body of Christ in the area, great opportunities for unity will undoubtedly arise.
5. Repent first to God for the sin against Him. All sin is transgression against God, so ask Him first. Then let there be repentance to the people (or descendants of the people) who were sinned against. If you are remitting sins of settlers against the Sioux Indians, for instance, it is best to have a descendant of the settlers and a Sioux, or someone who is part Sioux, to represent each side. The representatives should come forward and face each other. In the sight of the whole congregation, the people group who sinned should ask forgiveness of the people group against whom they sinned. Looking them in the eye, they should say something like this: "On behalf of my people, will you forgive us for . . . ?" Be as specific as possible. The person repre-

senting the group sinned against should look the other person in the eye and say, "On behalf of my people, we forgive you for. . . ." Again, be as specific as possible. Usually there is sin on both sides, such as prejudice or anger. Be sure both sides repent and forgive to the degree that is fitting.

There is no way to describe the tears, travail, joy and release that come from the remitting of sins! It seems to drain the anger from the oppressed people, release the shame of the people group who did the oppressing and shut a gate of hell in that area.

Praise God for the blood of Jesus Christ that was shed for the remission of sin and is powerful enough to bring healing to *your* city and nation!

## Another Miracle in Hemet

I have already recounted that when I first arrived in Hemet, it did not strike me as a lush valley with great agricultural potential. The Hemet valley was a dry, arid place that looked and felt like a desert. But I came to discover that this had not always been the case.

The valley, I learned, had once had plenty of water. In fact, the name *Hemet* is an Indian word meaning "hemmed in by trees." The valley had been so fertile that great orchards grew twelve hundred feet up the hillsides, all fed by natural springs. I have seen photographs of ranchers getting water in the early 1900s. A rancher would go out into his field with a pipe three or four inches in diameter and jam it the ground. Soon water would start bubbling up through the pipe and he could water his cattle. That is how high and easily accessible the water table around Hemet once was.

But during the 1930s, a water company decided to export water from the valley out to the surrounding communities. In order to do this, officials of the company needed to construct a water line, either built over the mountains or drilled through the mountains. They decided to drill. But company engineers miscalculated the direction of the pipe through the mountain and mistakenly tapped the underground water table, which did not legally belong to them.

Water gushed out of the mountain day after day, month after month. In fact, for more than a year, billions of gallons of water flowed out of the mountain. Company officials told ranchers and local residents that they were trying to stop the flow of water. But they were accused of diverting the water down a riverbed and selling it in neighboring Riverside and Orange Counties at a tremendous profit.

By the time the flow was finally stopped, the water table had been destroyed. The orchards began to die and ranchers were left hard-pressed. The worst agricultural destruction of all happened on the Soboba Indian Reservation. The Sobobas lost their only source of livelihood as the ground dried up and seemed to die.

So angry were the Sobobas at the water company that they called on their tribal shamans to curse the company and the workers on the water line. As the shamans began their curses, company workers actually began to die under inexplicable circumstances, including through bizarre accidents.

### Mending the Breach

Fifty years later The Dwelling Place of Hemet recognized that the relationship between the Sobobas and the white people of the valley was a major unhealed wound—a complex problem with sin on both sides that affected our community greatly. So we decided to remit the sins publicly through a solemn assembly. Cindy Jacobs, an anointed facilitator for solemn assemblies, joined us in Hemet one evening in September 1991 as we moved to bring forgiveness into the situation.

A Soboba Christian living on the reservation, along with the sister of the tribal chief, came to the solemn assembly to represent the tribe. They were seeking forgiveness for the curses of their shamans on the white man, so that as that sin was remitted, they would gain legal spiritual authority to break the curse. A current employee of the water company, a Christian young man, came to extend forgiveness toward the Sobobas and ask forgiveness for the sin of his company that had caused the problem in the first place.

As we gathered at The Dwelling Place for this solemn assembly, a gentleman in the very back of the church jumped up and came to the front. He was a missionary to Argentina, he told us, and he was home in Hemet for a two-week furlough. Unbelievably, he was one of the original water company workers fifty years earlier who had actually worked on the water line when the water table in the mountain was tapped. God had brought him all the way from Argentina to remit the sin of a company he had worked for in his youth!

Many in the congregation were moved to tears that evening as representatives from each side stood and, in the name of Jesus, asked forgiveness of one another. As the Sobobas and the water company representatives embraced and the tears flowed, I could feel the power of the enemy breaking. Sins on both sides had been washed away by the blood of Jesus, and Satan's legal right in the situation had been removed.

### Resulting Victories

Since that night we have seen tremendous victories for God's Kingdom in Hemet, with the Gospel making significant inroads in the Soboba tribe. Shortly after that event, opportunities for us to minister on the reservation began to open in unprecedented ways.

A weekly Bible study begun in a home on the reservation gave the Soboba Christians the tools they needed to begin reaching out to their fellow Sobobas. Eventually the believers began holding powerful revival meetings, which have been going on for some years now and which have borne great fruit. Other Native American tribes in the area have invited the Sobobas to minister on their reservations as well—ministry that has been richly blessed.

And shortly after we remitted the sins of the water company and the Sobobas, a man prepared to serve as a third-generation shaman made a public confession of faith at The Dwelling Place. His grandfather had been considered the most powerful shaman of all the surrounding tribes, as well as among the Cahuilla nation. We have been told (although we have no documentation) that his grandfather, acknowledged as head shaman in the 1930s, was one of the shamans who participated in cursing the water company workers. In any case, since shamanism was so deeply entrenched in this man's family's life, his conversion was nothing short of miraculous.

He has made tremendous progress in his Christian life. At the time of this writing, he is head usher at The Dwelling Place and participating in our pastoral training program.

Many Sobobas are now believers. It is incredible to see a twentieth-century Nineveh right here in our valley! And since the remitting of those sins in 1991, we have seen a literal healing of our land, following the principle of 2 Chronicles 7:14:

> "If My people who are called by My name will humble themselves, and pray and seek My face, and turn from their wicked ways, then I will hear from heaven, and will forgive their sin and heal their land."

How has God healed our land? Through an incredible restoration of water in our valley! We have enjoyed record rain levels in the years since the sins were remitted. While the water table is not back up to its original levels, the water in the streams, according to forestry workers who manage the San Bernardino National Forest nearby, flows better than it has since the 1930s.

And something even more miraculous shows how the blessing of God has returned (as God promises in 2 Chronicles 7:14) to the *physical* land that was defiled through this sin. In 1995 Southern California was allocated funds to produce the largest single water reservoir in all of California. This reservoir, they promised, would be larger than all the bodies of fresh water in Southern California put together. And where did the authorities choose as the site for this largest manmade body of fresh water in Southern California but our community of Hemet! What a miracle! A geologist told me that this reservoir, which is now under construction, will increase the level of the water table substantially.

Can God use reservoirs to heal the land? Of course He can! I believe that because God's people humbled themselves and asked forgiveness of Him and one another for corporate sin, God is now blessing both the people and the land in the community of Hemet.

In the final chapter of this book, let's look at the role of the local church, *your* church, as the catalyst for redemption in your community.

# 10
# The Key to Territorial Redemption

When spider webs unite, they can tie up a lion.
Helen Miller

Our ultimate objective in strategic-level spiritual warfare (as I pointed out in chapter 2) is not to know more secrets about our cities. Nor do we engage in spiritual mapping simply to have greater insight into the works of Satan within our communities. Our *only* interest in knowing what our enemy is up to is helping to establish God's purposes where we live. The cry of my heart, as I have said, is, "Your Kingdom come, Your will be done in my city as it is in heaven!"

No institution or ministry can replace the local church in accomplishing this objective. In fact, local churches are the key to territorial redemption and the major outposts of the Kingdom of God on earth.

An outpost, according to *Webster's Dictionary,* is a station established to protect an army from surprise attack. So, spiritually speaking, if we go into a region, neutralize demonic forces

144

and activate the local church as God intends, we will not only win the battle at hand but be ready to meet the enemy as he mounts new attacks against the Kingdom of God in that region.

Local churches should also be places of refuge, light, healing and guidance for the communities they serve. A church member whose pastor has made a territorial commitment to the city is as committed to its welfare as he or she is to the church itself.

## The Role of the Local Church

As an organization, the local church should be conveying to the community that it is there to serve and help. Too often the vision we have for our churches is unbalanced because we are not as committed to our cities as we are to our churches. Taking the commitment to a city out of a church diminishes the purpose of the church. We must ask ourselves, *Am I as committed to seeing my city prosper and grow as I am to seeing my church prosper and grow?* Only when the two come together do we have the makings of great territorial vision.

As a pastor, I like to think of it this way: A true shepherd has a heart for the community because we see its residents as future sheep. The community is the flock; the church members are just close friends.

### *Our Greatest Asset*

While members may be close friends, they are also a church's greatest asset. It is not the organization that will win souls for Christ or accomplish the task God has set before it. Those things are done by the people in the church. Pastors committed to the community need people who will understand and share in that vision.

The value of people within a local church is difficult to over-estimate. Without people, after all, there would be no church. Nevertheless, when a church is involved in matters of spiritual warfare, the need for a committed core of mature believers increases considerably. Pastors cannot implement a territorial vision alone. For pastors with a vision for the community, making a commitment to develop and lead the congregation to maturity is a necessary and worthwhile investment.

Leadership development expert John Maxwell, who served as a local church pastor for many years, has this to say: "The more people you develop, the greater the extent of your dreams."[1] Maxwell goes on to list some key points that "people-developers" need to understand:

> The one who influences others to lead is a leader without limitations.
> People tend to become what the most important people in their lives think they will become.
> People do not care how much you know until they know how much you care.
> Failure is the opportunity to begin again more intelligently.
> People do what people see.[2]

One of the greatest factors in motivating people, believes Maxwell, is helping them realize they can make a significant contribution to a cause that will have lasting impact. They need to see that what they are doing is not wasted effort.[3]

If a pastor can understand and communicate a God-given vision for his or her church and city, and understand and communicate the true value of each individual in implementing the vision, that pastor will have tapped into the church's greatest asset—a motivated congregation ready to see the Kingdom of God come to their city.

### *The Importance of Unity*

But even with a great vision and motivated congregation, no one church can win the whole city for Christ. Nor should it try! God uses a great spectrum of denominations to reach different segments of society. We should never be like the two fleas fighting over who owns the dog. We need each other to complete the Great Commission, even within our own communities.

In his book *Primary Purpose*, Ted Haggard provides this perspective:

> Inside the walls of our churches, let's teach and practice the full menu of what we believe.
>
> . . . But outside the walls of the church, I believe we must focus on the absolutes. Because when we do, we put tremendous pressure on the forces of evil that want to divide us and distract us from our primary purpose.
>
> The result is that the non-Christian community hears the same basic absolutes from thousands of Christians from a variety of churches. They start wondering where all the Christians have come from. In their viewpoint many people are talking about how wonderful Christ is and how great the Bible is. No longer are they hearing that Baptists are better than Presbyterians or that charismatics are more spiritual than Lutherans. They hear, instead, from all of those groups that Jesus is the only solution to the problems they face and that they can trust in the Bible.[4]

The good news is, unity is increasing exponentially in the Body of Christ! With the help of interdenominational movements such as Marches for Jesus, Concerts of Prayer, Promise Keepers and the A.D. 2000 & Beyond Movement, Christians are learning that we can honor one another without the former trappings of jealousy and suspicion. Churches within the Body of Christ can share in the same goals, and even work together, without losing the distinctives of their particular affiliation or denomination.

## Pastors as Gatekeepers

Ecclesiastical unity in any community is crucial to seeing that city won for Christ. Achieving unity among churches, however, stands or falls on the pastors of that community.

I referred in the last chapter to pastors in a city as spiritual gatekeepers, and as such they have been given divine authority in the city.

## *Their Authority*

In fact, pastors within a city have more spiritual authority within their community than any other Christian. Few of us would question how spiritually strategic Billy Graham has been for decades in the Kingdom of God. But the local pastors in Montreat, North Carolina, have more authority in that town than Billy Graham, who is a resident there. The pastors of that town are God's spiritual gatekeepers and, as such, carry more spiritual authority in that city than Billy Graham, a traveling evangelist.

Let's take a look at what Peter taught about pastoral authority:

> The *elders* who are among you I exhort, I who am a fellow elder and a witness of the sufferings of Christ, and also a partaker of the glory that will be revealed: *Shepherd* the flock of God which is among you, serving as *overseers*, not by compulsion but willingly, not for dishonest gain but eagerly.
>
> 1 Peter 5:1–2 (italics added)

This is the only passage in the Bible in which the following three Greek words appear together: elders (*presbuterion*), shepherd (*poimen*) and overseers (*episkopos*). These are synonyms for the modern-day office of pastor.

Later in this chapter Peter tells us, "Likewise you younger people, submit yourselves to your elders *[presbuteros]*. Yes, all of you be submissive to one another, and be clothed with humility . . ." (1 Peter 5:5). Peter is not advocating spiritual anarchy in exhorting us to be submissive to one another. On the contrary, he is referring to a biblical order of submission both at home (see 1 Peter 3:1–12) and in the church, with pastors holding a unique position of authority.[5]

## *Their Responsibility*

Along with any true authority comes responsibility. Gatekeepers of a city hold spiritual responsibilities that go along with their position. Two responsibilities in particular, out of many that pastors have, relate to their role as gatekeepers.

### 1. REMITTING THE SINS OF THE CITY

Pastors are held accountable, as spiritual gatekeepers of a city, for issues that affect the spiritual condition of the region. God has set pastors as spiritual commanders of the outposts of the Kingdom of God. This gives pastors certain responsibilities within the city in which their church (or outpost) is located.

In Deuteronomy 21:1–9 we read an illustration of clerical responsibility in a region. In this passage the Lord gave specific instructions as to how a dead body found outside a city was to be dealt with if no murderer could be identified. The Levitical priests were to measure physically to determine the city closest to the dead body. Then that city was held accountable in the eyes of God for the murder, and an appropriate sacrifice had to be made in order to remit the sin of innocent bloodshed. This was the way God prescribed to wash the guilt of that sin from a city.

Because of the blood of Jesus, priests and pastors no longer need to make sacrifices on an altar on behalf of a city. But the city still needs cleansing from the sins for which God holds it accountable. Pastors, like Levitical priests, occupy a unique position to cry out to God for forgiveness on behalf of their cities. It is their responsibility and right to apply the blood of Jesus to the guilt of their cities, which, under the New Covenant, is done through prayer.

### 2. REMITTING THE SINS OF THE CHURCH

When churches in a city are guilty of sectarianism and worship of pet doctrines, we sin not only against one another, but against our community. Pastors are both responsible and anointed to remit these sins.

A few years back, pastors in Hemet took responsibility for our own sectarianism. A cross-section of evangelical, charismatic and Pentecostal pastors gathered for a special service one evening in which we apologized publicly to the community for the division between us. Then we asked forgiveness of one another for specific things.

At one point a Methodist pastor stepped onto the platform and asked forgiveness of a Pentecostal pastor for treating that church as if it represented the lunatic fringe because its members spoke in tongues. Tears flowed as the Pentecostal pastor turned and asked forgiveness for his own sin of treating the Methodists as second-class Christians because they did *not* speak in tongues.

Soon after that night, the pastors' fellowship in our town began to blossom and thrive, as we began seeing one another as friends and peers rather than "the competition down the street." And since that service, sectarianism has lost its power in Hemet.

## Help for the Gatekeepers

While pastors are spiritual gatekeepers of a city, they alone cannot always know what the enemy is up to. Furthermore, pastors are often the target of enemy assault. The fact is, pastors need help in being effective gatekeepers, and God in His mercy has provided special groups of people gifted to help them do just that. Here are two.

### *Watchmen on the Walls*

God has gifted one special group of people to help pastors discern the spiritual climate of their cities and to provide a shield around pastors and their families against onslaughts of the enemy. These people are the intercessors, whom God has placed as guards, or "watchmen on the walls," for the pastor, the church and the community.

Listen to what God said through Isaiah: "I have set watchmen on your walls, O Jerusalem; they shall never hold their peace day or night" (Isaiah 62:6). And to Ezekiel He said: "Son of man, I have made you a watchman for the house of Israel; therefore hear a word from My mouth, and give them warning from Me" (Ezekiel 3:17).

It is a wise pastor who understands and encourages the intercessors of the congregation to use their God-given gifts to help him or her fulfill the position of gatekeeper.[6]

### The Hidden Eldership

Others in a community can also offer great help to the gatekeepers. John Dawson identifies a certain group that he calls "hidden eldership":

> Identify your city's prophets, intercessors and spiritual elders. In every city there is what I call a hidden eldership—a group of saints that you will not find listed in any book. It consists of God's circle of mature believers who "stand in the gap" until victory comes. . . . Some of these "watchmen" are obvious, such as veteran pastors. Others may be intercessors in obscurity or prophetic people with a premonition. If there is a common theme among those who are sensitive to the Spirit's guidance, you're on to something. God always confirms a strategy through several witnesses, and this is particularly important when dealing with demonic forces.[7]

Spiritual gatekeepers of a city need not feel they are alone in the task God has given them. Both the watchmen and the hidden eldership in the church have been provided by God to bring discernment and wisdom to assist gatekeepers in their task of advancing the Kingdom of God in their community.

## Beyond the Walls of Our Churches

Pastors must be willing to venture outside the four secure walls of their congregations and do in public what they do in private. They must be willing to minister *to* their communities in tangible ways, to let people see and feel and experience Christ's love through us, the living Church.

Here are a few examples of how The Dwelling Place has reached out into our own community of Hemet:

- *Hallelujah Night.* Each year we hold our annual Hallelujah Night, an evening aimed at getting children off dark streets on Halloween night and into a safe Christian environment. What kid would choose trick-or-treating for candy when he or she can ride ponies, take a train ride, play large, outdoor, carnival-type games, bounce around in a moon bounce, *plus* take home oodles of candy? The event keeps growing every year. This year twelve hundred people turned out for this community event.
- *Chaplain's Program.* I have become involved in the Hemet Chaplain's Program to assist police and firemen when needed. Many hurt people have been ministered to by local pastors through this vital program.
- *Canning Hunger Food Program.* For the past two years we committed ourselves to collect food each month for the hungry in our valley. The food was dispensed through the local Salvation Army.
- *The Hemet Christmas Parade.* The Dwelling Place has entered the local Hemet Christmas Parade for the past nine years, taking anywhere from 350 to 500 people from our congregation down the main streets of our city declaring that Jesus is Lord. Every church body should be celebrating the birth of our Savior with the biggest and best birthday party of the year! So we enter a huge float with our worship team, singers, choreographed dancers, flag-carriers, camels, horses, banners and our happy congregation, all wishing the parade-watchers a merry and joyful Christmas and showing our city the real and lasting meaning of Christmas. Eight first-place trophies attest to the fact that a church can produce a quality entry and lift up the mighty name of Jesus at the same time.

- *Holiday Food Outreach.* This program is coordinated on either Thanksgiving or Christmas. Each year the congregation delivers between 200 and 250 complete dinners, often including gifts for children and lighted Christmas trees to families in our community.

I recount these few outreaches and programs only to give you some examples. Church size is not the issue here. You do not have to be big or wealthy to reach out and touch the lifestream of your own community in tangible ways.

What are the needs in your community, and where are the open doors for your church to meet those needs?

## Donkey Experiences

I mentioned in chapter 2 a definition of insanity as doing something the same way you have always done it and expecting to see new results. But too often churches are afraid of trying new things. What if we make a mistake?

Well, contrary to popular belief, I think there are not two but three guarantees in life: death, taxes and your next mistake! Mistakes are nothing to be afraid of; we *will* make them. A much more frightening prospect is the status quo, especially when we realize that people in our communities are going to hell every day of the week because Satan has blinded them from responding to the Gospel.

As we engage in strategic-level warfare for our communities, we may experience things we have never heard of before. At times we will have no precedent or even paradigm for what is going on around us.

A classic biblical example of such an occasion is when Balaam's donkey talked to him. As Balaam beat his donkey, angrily urging her onward (see Numbers 22:22–35), the donkey warned the prophet of impending doom if they took one more step. And the donkey was right!

Prior to the time of Balaam, there was no precedent for a donkey talking. There was even less for listening to one! Nevertheless, God used *that* donkey in *that* way at *that* time. To the best of my knowledge, He has not used a donkey in the same way since. Can He do it again? Of course. But as far as I know, He hasn't.

We cannot expect new results from doing the same things we have done for years. We must be willing to stretch, to try things that may be new to us as we intercede for our communities. Peter Wagner describes several new methods that the Body of Christ has begun using to help tear the walls down between churches and communities. These include *praise marches*, which are focused on cities; *prayer walks*, which are focused on neighborhoods; *prayer expeditions*, which are focused on regions; and *prayer journeys*, which are focused on strongholds.[8]

As we move into activities like these, as well as spiritual mapping, identificational repentance and strategic-level intercession, we may have some donkey experiences along the way!

### *One Sunday Afternoon*

A few years ago I began to sense the importance of praying not only *for* but *in* a community. One Sunday in July 1988, I felt the time had come to give it a try. During the morning services I announced to our congregation a special time of prayer in our community. I asked them to give up lunch and meet that afternoon up in the parking lot of the Ramona Bowl, a hillside amphitheater that overlooks the Hemet valley.

I was pleasantly surprised by the number of people who showed up that Sunday afternoon to pray for Hemet. We rimmed the entire edge of the parking lot, person next to person, arms extended and lifted in prayer over the entire Hemet valley.

That Sunday afternoon prayer was a moving experience for me, and the first time many people there had ever prayed like that in public. Many said later they felt that their lives had been changed as a result. Many more began to feel a new burden to pray for the community.

I cannot say truthfully that one prayer time alone changed our community. But it did change our church.

## *Raising Our Prayer Canopy*

Three years later, on a Sunday morning in August 1991, I woke up well before five A.M. As I lay in bed, unusually awake, the Lord gave me a phenomenal set of instructions.

*Set up a prayer canopy over the valley,* He said. *Place an elder at the four main entrances of the valley—north, south, east and west. Have each of them take a three-foot wooden stake and inscribe on it Isaiah 33:20–24. You, Bob, are to go to the main intersection of the valley and lift a public offering of praise at exactly the same time that each elder is driving a stake into the ground at the four points of the valley. As you lift up the offering of praise, you will be raising the center pole of a canopy of intercession over the valley, and the stakes will represent the four corners of the canopy. You are to do this today at five P.M., and you are to make this opportunity available to all in the congregation.*

Taken aback by this message from God, I opened my Bible to Isaiah:

> Look upon Zion, the city of our appointed feasts; your eyes will see Jerusalem, a quiet home, a tabernacle that will not be taken down; not one of its stakes will ever be removed, nor will any of its cords be broken. But there the majestic LORD will be for us a place of broad rivers and streams, in which no galley with oars will sail, nor majestic ships pass by (for the LORD is our Judge, the LORD is our Lawgiver, the LORD is our King; He will save us); Your tackle is loosed, they could not strengthen their mast, they could not spread the sail.
>
> Then the prey of great plunder is divided; the lame take the prey. And the inhabitant will not say, "I am sick"; the people who dwell in it will be forgiven their iniquity.
>
> Isaiah 33:20–24

I did not begin to understand the significance of the nautical references, which did not seem to relate to our landlocked, desert community of Hemet. Still, it was a passage depicting salvation and stability for a land, and I felt a sense of excitement about this prophetic act of prayer.

My first step that Sunday morning was to contact the elders and explain to them what I was sensing from the Lord. After some discussion, prior to the two morning worship services, we all agreed we would rather err on the side of faith than on the side of doubt. One elder agreed to go home and make the stakes that afternoon, similar to the ones we had used at Massacre Canyon and on the Soboba reservation.

Now I had a challenge before me: How to convey this message to the congregation without sounding like a kook to our guests and visitors?

In both services I announced simply that we would gather that afternoon at 4:30 to set up a prayer canopy at five o'clock over our valley. Then we would return for the evening service at six, discuss the events of our afternoon journeys and include a time of prayer for the valley.

To my surprise, more than 150 people showed up at 4:30 P.M. ready to pray for their community. We divided into five equal groups and headed to our respective locations.

At exactly five P.M., while all four elders were driving their stakes into the ground and reading the passage from Isaiah aloud, Susan and I led our group in offering praise at the main intersection in town (which happens to be centrally located in the valley). It was intimidating to do this as traffic passed and people gawked, but I could feel a sense of destiny on us for our valley.

At six, when we all returned for the evening service, three of the four elders shared what their groups had experienced during the times of intercession. Everyone was deeply moved by their prayer for the community, though perplexed as to why the verses in Isaiah referred to a ship's tackle (or rigging) and mast and sails.

Don Hales was the last elder to share. I could hear something different in his tone, and he had a look on his face as if he knew something we did not.

He began by explaining that his group had been assigned to the north end of the valley, and that the location had something in common with the passage from Isaiah 33:

> Your eyes will see . . . a tabernacle that will not be taken down; not one of its *stakes* will ever be removed. . . . But there the majestic LORD will be for us a place of *broad rivers and streams*. . . .
>
> verses 20–21 (italics added)

The group, Don explained enthusiastically, had been standing on the bank of the San Jacinto River, and to their immediate left was the stream running out of Massacre Canyon. They had prayed alongside a river *and* a stream.

We had not chosen their location for this reason, although the similarity was certainly interesting. But why would this be so exciting to them as a form of spiritual confirmation?

Don went on to explain that the group had sensed the Lord instructing them at the end of their prayer time to return to the church another way. So they took the road that crosses the stream to the east, past the property belonging to the Church of Scientology. And on that property, directly adjacent to the stream bed, they were stunned to see a prominent construction of a full-scale mast of a ship, along with sail and rigging!

So *that* was the connection with the verses in Isaiah 33 mentioning the mast, rigging and sail of a ship:

> But there the majestic LORD will be for us a place of broad rivers and streams, in which *no galley with oars will sail, nor majestic ships pass by. . . . Your tackle is loosed, they could not strengthen their mast, they could not spread the sail.*
>
> Then the prey of great plunder is divided; the lame take the prey.
>
> verses 21, 23 (italics added)

What, after all, were the odds of finding a full-scale ship's mast and rigging in the desert? This was no accident or fluke. We all sensed through this scriptural confirmation that "great plunder" had indeed been divided, and that we had struck a strategic blow for the Kingdom of God in our area.

Soon after we completed this prophetic act, the flow of information about the activity of darkness in our community increased dramatically. Shedding light on Satan's secrets, as I said in chapter 8, leads to our enemy's greatest weakness—his battle plans exposed. And the members of The Dwelling Place saw a definite correlation between our obedience to God and the exposure of darkness in our community.

Since that Sunday in August 1991, churches in our community who want to reach the lost have seen dramatic change. At The Dwelling Place, people have responded to invitations to salvation almost every Sunday, with the exception of fewer than ten occasions.

## How Hemet Has Been Changed

I trust you have gotten the idea that the principles I have been discussing throughout this book have had a tremendous impact on Hemet. I would like to conclude this book by giving a few examples of how three activities in particular—commitment to the land, spiritual mapping and strategic-level spiritual warfare—have changed our city.

### Unity Across Denominational Boundaries

I have stressed the importance of unity among members of a church and pastors in a community. The reason I know unity is important is because I have experienced disunity within Hemet. Pastors here saw one another as competitors, maintaining a suspicious, distant attitude, even passing each other in retail stores and pretending to not see one another. But since coming to understand the importance of unity and commitment, we have used tools like identificational and personal repentance to bridge the wide gap.

Earlier in this chapter I explained that a cross-section of evangelical, charismatic and Pentecostal pastors gathered for a special service in which we apologized publicly to the community for the divisions between us. God has honored these and other efforts and worked a miracle of unity among us. Pastors who were once at great odds with one another have become good friends, enjoying the relationship of peers, some even sharing pulpits on Sunday mornings. One pastor in the community asked me recently to dedicate his new child. "Behold, how good and how pleasant it is for brethren to dwell together in unity!" (Psalm 133:1).

Unity in leadership has also spread across denominational lines. In 1991 the pastors of our valley, including Pentecostal, charismatic, mainline and evangelical, had our first interdenominational tent revival. Thirty-five churches and their pastors came together every night for two weeks, with a different pastor and musical group ministering together each night on the platform. The combination flowed beautifully. One night, for instance, a Pentecostal worship team and a Baptist pastor ministered. Every night of those two weeks, the tent was full. And by the end of that time, many people had been saved, healed and delivered as a result of the unity of the Body of Christ in our valley.

We have now formed an interdenominational pastors' fellowship that meets every Thursday morning to pray over the community, minister to one another and build relationships with each other. Denominational boundaries have grown less and less important as we have each made a commitment to the community and a commitment to serve one another in the love of Christ.

## Gang Members Finding New Life

I mentioned earlier that Hemet is known as a sleepy retirement community. Even so, the valley in which Hemet is located has long had problems with gangs and gang violence. In the 1990s graffiti, the most visible sign of gang activity, was everywhere. One church in a particularly bad section, pastored by my good friend Gordon Housten, had a team of seven or eight people who painted the walls of the church *every day* in order to cover the previous night's graffiti.

It was when our intercession teams were praying about the gang situation that we sensed the Lord giving us the strategy of driving stakes into the ground and raising a canopy of prayer over our community. Since that time, some incredible changes have taken place in the gang situation.

The same church that had to paint its walls every day developed a special, Holy Spirit-empowered effectiveness in ministering to gangs. One Sunday morning in 1993, during the worship service, a young man who lived across the street and was a leader in a violent gang came walking down the aisle right in the middle of the sermon. The pastor was understandably nervous as this hardened gang member walked straight toward him! But as he approached, the pastor could see in his eyes that he meant no harm.

The young man stopped in front of the congregation and said, "I'm sorry to interrupt you, but I know if I don't give my life to Christ today, I'm going to die. I don't want to die. What do I have to do?"

The pastor, joining him, guided him in a prayer.

From that day on, the graffiti stopped. The young man told his gang he had accepted Christ, that he liked that pastor and that no one should touch his property again. Not only did the graffiti stop, but the members of the gang began guarding the church, becoming a security force in that tough neighborhood. And since then, many other gang members have accepted Christ and joined that church.

## A New Security Force

In the months that followed, the church started having bizarre disruptions during worship services. One Sunday morning, for instance, a woman came into the sanctuary in the middle of the service wearing only a terrycloth robe that was not closed in front. Carrying a baby doll and a blanket, she walked right down the center aisle and sat down in the front row. Needless to say, it was difficult to refocus on worship that day!

Overall it was clear something was wrong. The intercessors of the church, provoked to warfare prayer, asked God to reveal why these incidents were happening with some frequency.

Then one night the pastor got a call from the police department asking him to come down to the church right away. The gang had spotted something and reported it to the police. When the pastor arrived, he was met with an unusual story. The gang had caught a prostitute climbing up the barred windows to the roof of the church with one of her patrons. She had set up a mattress and little butane stove and was doing business on the roof right over the pulpit. Talk about looking in the unobvious places!

The intercessors of the church bound the perverse spirits that had been gaining access to the church building through prostitution. And immediately the bizarre occurrences stopped. God had used the former gang members to answer the prayers of the intercessors and expose a stronghold of the enemy.

### An Unexpected Answer to Prayer

In 1996, once we began implementing the principles of strategic-level warfare and asking the Lord to expose any hidden darkness within our community, God answered our prayer in an unexpected way.

Several weeks after a young man accepted Christ in our church, he began feeling guilty because he knew about something going on in the community that no one else knew about. He told me he had been working at an illegal drug lab that was producing methamphetamine, or speed.

It was no small operation. Hemet, as we came to find out, was the methamphetamine capital of the West Coast. Several such labs had been producing hundreds of pounds of the illegal drug every month. Pure methamphetamine powder was being disguised as 4x8 sheets of drywall, with the powder tucked neatly between gray drywall paper, and truckloads of this "drywall" were being shipped up and down the West Coast. The Drug Enforcement Agency was notified of the situation and given information that resulted in the disruption of drug manufacturing and trafficking in our community.

We would never have guessed what was really going on in our city unless God exposed it. So as you enter into strategic-level intercession and ask God to reveal problem areas in your community, be prepared to learn surprising things and see Him move in unexpected ways.

The gang problem in our community is not completely gone, but it is much improved. We believe that through strategic-level intercession, the Church of Jesus Christ in Hemet has broken through a barrier. We believe God for great things to continue happening within the gangs of our community.

## A Final Word

In this book I have only begun to tell how commitment to the land, followed by spiritual mapping and strategic-level intercession, has helped to change our community of Hemet, California. Much, much more has happened in our city. But more important, as pastors and laypersons learn these principles and apply them in their own communities, stories of victory over Satan are surfacing all over.

Strategic-level intercession works, and the local church is the key to territorial redemption. Though it requires costly commitment, it bears everlasting fruit for the Kingdom of God and allows us to leave a godly legacy for future generations. If the Lord does not come back during our lifetimes, I pray that God will give us the grace to bring a greater measure of His Kingdom to our communities. Proverbs 13:22 says, "A good man leaves an inheritance to his children's children."

Let us do the work we are called to, including building the Kingdom of God in our communities, so that our children and their children and their children after them will pick up the banner gladly and carry on until Christ returns for His Bride.

# Notes

### Chapter 1: Hemet Calls!

1. Louis L'Amour, *The Lonesome Gods* (New York: Bantam, 1983), p. 45.

### Chapter 2: Maximizing the Power of Intercession

1. For further study on this topic, see C. Peter Wagner, ed., *Breaking Strongholds in Your City* (Ventura, Calif.: Regal, 1993), chapter 2, "The Visible and the Invisible."

2. For further study see Kjell Sjoberg, *Winning the Prayer War* (Chichester, England: New Wine Press, 1991).

3. Ed Silvoso, *That None Should Perish* (Ventura, Calif.: Regal, 1994), p. 53.

### Chapter 3: The Earth Is the Lord's

1. C. I. Scofield, ed., *The New Scofield Study Bible* (Nashville: Thomas Nelson, 1989), p. 5, note 2.

2. Kenneth L. Barker & John Kohlenberger III, eds., *Zondervan NIV Bible Commentary: Volume 2: New Testament* (Grand Rapids: Zondervan, 1994), p. 691.

3. R. V. G. Tasker, *The Second Epistle of Paul to the Corinthians, An Introduction and Commentary* (Grand Rapids: Eerdmans, 1958), pp. 140–141.

### Chapter 5: Understand Your Community

1. Christian Broadcasting Network, *Light the Window* videotape (Virginia Beach, Va., 1995).

2. John Dawson, *Taking Our Cities for God* (Lake Mary, Fla.: Creation House, 1989), p. 39.

3. Ibid., p. 40.

## Chapter 7: Can a Whole City Be Influenced Demonically?

1. C. S. Lewis, *The Screwtape Letters* (New York: Macmillan, 1961).

2. Noel C. Gibson, *The Gospel Overcomes Satanic Oppression* (Drummoyne, Australia: Freedom in Christ Ministries Trust, 1994), pp. 84–85.

3. C. Peter Wagner, *Warfare Prayer* (Ventura, Calif.: Regal, 1992), p. 96.

4. The following references (listed alphabetically) were used in compiling this list and are excellent resources for further study on demonization:

Noel and Phyl Gibson, *Deliver Our Children from the Evil One* (Kent, England: Sovereign World, 1992).

———, *Evicting Demonic Intruders* (West Sussex, England: New Wine Press, 1993).

Frank Hammond, *Demons and Deliverance in the Ministry of Jesus* (Plainview, Tex.: The Children's Bread Ministry, 1991).

Frank and Ida Mae Hammond, *Pigs in the Parlor* (Kirkwood, Mo.: Impact Books, 1973).

Charles Kraft, *Defeating Dark Angels* (Ann Arbor, Mich.: Servant, 1992).

Ed Murphy, *The Handbook for Spiritual Warfare* (Nashville: Thomas Nelson, 1992).

John and Paula Sandford, *Healing the Wounded Spirit* (South Plainfield, N.J.: Bridge Publishing, 1985).

Doris M. Wagner, "Understanding Basic Issues in Deliverance" seminar, Global Harvest Ministries, Colorado Springs, Colo., December 1995.

John Wimber, *Power Healing* (San Francisco: Harper & Row, 1987).

5. Murphy, *Handbook*, p. 442.

6. Gibson, *Demonic Intruders,* chapter 10.

7. Kraft, *Dark Angels,* pp. 70–71.

8. Ibid., pp. 73–74.

9. Ibid., pp. 75–76.

10. George Otis, Jr., "An Overview of Spiritual Mapping," Wagner, *Breaking Strongholds,* p. 40.

11. J. Edward Decker, Jr., *The Question of Freemasonry,* a booklet published by Free the Masons Ministries, P.O. Box 1077, Issaquah, WA 98027.

12. Otis, "An Overview," p. 41.

13. Ibid., pp. 41–42.

## Chapter 8: Stronger than the Strongman

1. Ted Haggard, *Primary Purpose* (Lake Mary, Fla.: Creation House, 1995), p. 159.

2. Cindy Jacobs, *Possessing the Gates of the Enemy* (Grand Rapids: Chosen Books, 1991), p. 93.

3. Haggard, *Purpose*, pp. 56–60.

4. For those readers who would like an excellent resource on understanding, discovering and developing spiritual gifts, I strongly recommend the book by C. Peter Wagner *Your Spiritual Gifts Can Help Your Church Grow* (Ventura, Calif.: Regal, 1994). This book, an easy-to-understand, biblically based study, includes a 125-question spiritual gifts questionnaire designed to help any believer discover his or her spiritual gift(s).

5. John Dawson, *Taking Our Cities,* pp. 39, 41.

6. Jack W. Hayford, "Possessing Our Cities and Towns," *Engaging the Enemy*, C. Peter Wagner, ed. (Ventura, Calif.: Regal, 1991), p. 75.

## Chapter 9: A Call to Repentance

1. Cindy Jacobs, "Identificational Repentance through Biblical Remitting of Sins," *Releasing Destiny: A Spiritual Warfare Manual for Nashville and Country Music,* Stephen Mansfield, ed. (Nashville: Daniel 1 School of Leadership, 1993), pp. 49–52. This book is available through Daniel 1 School of Leadership, P.O. Box 293330, Nashville, TN 37229-3330.

2. F. F. Bruce, *The Books and the Parchments* (Westwood, N.J.: Fleming H. Revell, 1950), pp. 81–82.

3. Gary S. Greig, "Generational Sin and Confessing the Sins of One's Ancestors and Nation," Regent University memo, October 18, 1995, pp. 8–9.

4. Jacobs, "Identificational Repentance," pp. 51–52.

## Chapter 10: The Key to Territorial Redemption

1. John C. Maxwell, *Developing the Leader Within You* (Nashville: Thomas Nelson, 1993), p. 103.

2. Ibid., p. 105.

3. Ibid., p. 110.

4. Ted Haggard, *Primary Purpose* (Lake Mary, Fla.: Creation House, 1995), pp. 63–64.

5. Information paraphrased from a C. Peter Wagner lecture.

6. For further study on the topic of intercession for Christian leaders, I recommend C. Peter Wagner's *Prayer Shield: How to Intercede for Pastors, Christian Leaders and Others on the Spiritual Frontlines* (Regal, 1992). This book is written to both leader and intercessor.

7. John Dawson, "Seventh Time Around," *Engaging the Enemy*, pp. 140–141.

8. C. Peter Wagner, *Churches That Pray* (Ventura, Calif.: Regal, 1993), pp. 144–145.

# Recommended Reading

Anderson, Neil T., and Charles Mylander. *Setting Your Church Free.* Ventura, Calif.: Regal, 1994. 352 pp. How to do spiritual warfare on behalf of a congregation that may be under bondage to the forces of darkness.

Dawson, John. *Taking Our Cities for God.* Lake Mary, Fla.: Creation House, 1989. 219 pp. The first textbook on breaking spiritual strongholds over geographical areas and a pioneering examination of strategic-level spiritual warfare.

——. *Healing America's Wounds.* Ventura, Calif.: Regal, 1994. 280 pp. The first textbook on one of the most essential elements in strategic-level spiritual warfare: identificational repentance.

Haggard, Ted. *Primary Purpose.* Orlando, Fla.: Creation House, 1995. 178 pp. An excellent look by a local church pastor at how intercession can change the spiritual climate of a city.

Hawthorne, Steve, and Graham Kendrick. *Prayerwalking.* Orlando, Fla.: Creation House, 1993. 191 pp. A practical handbook on praying in the community, reflecting a significant wave of spiritual activity geared for the 1990s.

Jacobs, Cindy. *Possessing the Gates of the Enemy.* Tarrytown, N.Y.: Chosen, 1991. 271 pp. This book, which lives up to its subtitle, "A Training Manual for Militant Intercession," has a wealth of information found in no other source.

Murphy, Ed. *The Handbook for Spiritual Warfare.* Nashville: Thomas Nelson, 1992. 520 pp. The most exhaustive textbook available on spiritual warfare. Very strong on biblical material.

Otis, George, Jr. *The Last of the Giants.* Tarrytown, N.Y.: Chosen, 1991. 272 pp. A serious attempt to introduce spiritual mapping, enabling us to see the world around us as it really is, not as it appears to be. The author is a member of the Spiritual Warfare Network.

——. *Spiritual Mapping Field Guide.* The Sentinel Group (P.O. Box 6334, Lynnwood, WA 98036), 1993. 105 pp. A research methodology handbook for all who want to undertake projects involving spiritual mapping.

Pedersen, Bjorn. *Face to Face with God in Your Church: Establishing a Prayer Ministry.* Minneapolis: Augsburg, 1995. 111 pp. The most practical guide to installing a local church prayer ministry, written by one of the nation's top ministers of prayer, serving Community Church of Joy in Phoenix.

Sheets, Dutch. *Intercessory Prayer.* Ventura, Calif.: Regal, 1996. 275 pp. A clear, compelling look at prayer. Very strong theologically.

Silvoso, Edgardo. *That None Should Perish.* Ventura, Calif.: Regal, 1994. 291 pp. One of the books of the decade—the first textbook on "prayer evangelism" written by a member of the Spiritual Warfare Network.

Sjoberg, Kjell. *Winning the Prayer War.* New Wine Press (Box 17, Chichester, England PO20 6YB), 1991. 95 pp. The seasoned wisdom of one of today's most respected intercessors and practitioners of strategic-level spiritual warfare.

Vander Griend, Alvin J. *The Praying Church Sourcebook.* Church Development Resources (2850 Kalamazoo Ave. S.E., Grand Rapids, MI 49560), 1990. 270 pp. The most extensive idea book for prayer ministries in the local church.

Wagner, C. Peter, ed. *Engaging the Enemy: How to Fight and Defeat Territorial Spirits.* Ventura, Calif.: Regal, 1991. 202 pp. A collection of the writings of eighteen Christian leaders on the subject of strategic-level spiritual warfare. The editor is a member of the Spiritual Warfare Network.

——. *Warfare Prayer.* Ventura, Calif.: Regal, 1992. 197 pp. A concise presentation of biblical, anthropological and field ministry perspectives on strategic-level spiritual warfare.

——, ed. *Breaking Strongholds in Your City.* Ventura, Calif.: Regal, 1993. 232 pp. The first textbook on spiritual mapping for the average Christian. Contributors include George Otis, Jr., Cindy Jacobs, Kjell Sjoberg and several others.

———. *Prayer Shield*. Ventura, Calif.: Regal, 1992. 196 pp. The first book on how to intercede for pastors and other Christian leaders, written to link pastors with intercessors.

———. *Churches That Pray*. Ventura, Calif.: Regal, 1993. 233 pp. How prayer relates to the growth of the local church and why it is necessary to pray not only in the church but in the community.

———. *Confronting the Powers*. Ventura, Calif.: Regal, 1996. 272 pp. A strong biblical rationale for strategic-level spiritual warfare today based on lessons from the New Testament Church.

——— and F. Douglas Pennoyer, eds. *Wrestling with Dark Angels*. Ventura, Calif.: Regal, 1990. 347 pp. Material presented at a symposium of professors from evangelical and charismatic colleges and seminaries relating to power evangelism and the demonic.

White, Thomas B. *The Believer's Guide to Spiritual Warfare*. Ann Arbor, Mich.: Servant, 1990. 172 pp. Excellent material on our personal preparation for spiritual warfare.

———. *Breaking Strongholds*. Ann Arbor, Mich.: Servant, 1993. 217 pp. A companion volume to *The Believer's Guide to Spiritual Warfare* that deals with strongholds on all three levels of spiritual warfare: ground level, occult level and strategic level.

# Index

Bob Beckett, a leader with the Spiritual Warfare Network, the Generals of Intercession and the Reconciliation Coalition, pastors The Dwelling Place in Hemet, California, and travels extensively training pastors and intercessors. He also teaches for C. Peter Wagner on spiritual issues and church growth at Fuller Theological Seminary. Bob and his wife, Susan, have two married daughters, both involved in ministry.

For more information, write to

Pastor Bob Beckett
The Dwelling Place
27100 Girard
Hemet, CA 91544